MARY ROSE

MARY ROSE
A PLAY IN THREE ACTS

BY

J. M. BARRIE

Fredonia Books
Amsterdam, The Netherlands

Mary Rose:
(A Play in Three Acts)

by
J. M. Barrie

ISBN: 1-58963-710-0

Copyright © 2002 by Fredonia Books

Reprinted from the 1924 edition

Fredonia Books
Amsterdam, The Netherlands
http://www.fredoniabooks.com

All rights reserved, including the right to reproduce this book, or portions thereof, in any form.

In order to make original editions of historical works available to scholars at an economical price, this facsimile of the original edition of 1924 is reproduced from the best available copy and has been digitally enhanced to improve legibility, but the text remains unaltered to retain historical authenticity.

ACT I

ACT I

The scene is a room in a small Sussex manor house that has long been for sale. It is such a silent room that whoever speaks first here is a bold one, unless indeed he merely mutters to himself, which they perhaps allow. All of this room's past which can be taken away has gone. Such light as there is comes from the only window, which is at the back and is incompletely shrouded in sacking. For a moment this is a mellow light, and if a photograph could be taken quickly we might find a disturbing smile on the room's face, perhaps like the Monna Lisa's, which came, surely, of her knowing what only the dead should know. There are two doors, one leading downstairs; the other is at the back, very insignificant, though it is the centre of this disturbing history. The wall-paper, heavy in the adherence of other papers of a still older date, has peeled and leans forward here and there in a grotesque bow, as men have hung in chains; one might predict that the next sound heard here will be in the distant future when another piece of paper loosens. Save for two packing-cases, the only furni-

ture is a worn easy-chair doddering by the unlit fire, like some foolish old man. We might play with the disquieting fancy that this room, once warm with love, is still alive but is shrinking from observation, and that with our departure they cunningly set to again at the apparently never-ending search which goes on in some empty old houses.

Some one is heard clumping up the stair, and the caretaker enters. It is not she, however, who clumps; she has been here for several years, and has become sufficiently a part of the house to move noiselessly in it. The first thing we know about her is that she does not like to be in this room. She is an elderly woman of gaunt frame and with a singular control over herself. There may be some one, somewhere, who can make her laugh still, one never knows, but the effort would hurt her face. Even the war, lately ended, meant very little to her. She has shown a number of possible purchasers over the house, just as she is showing one over it now, with the true caretaker's indifference whether you buy or not. The few duties imposed on her here she performs conscientiously, but her greatest capacity is for sitting still in the dark. Her work over, her mind a blank, she sits thus rather than pay for a candle. One knows a little more about life when he knows the Mrs. Oterys, but she herself is unaware that she is peculiar, and probably thinks that in some such way do people in general pass the hour before bedtime. Nevertheless, though saving of her candle in other empty houses, she always lights it on the approach of evening in this one.

The man who has clumped up the stairs in her wake is a young Australian soldier, a private, such as in those days you met by the dozen in any London street, slouching along it forlornly if alone, with sudden stoppages to pass the time (in which you ran against him), or in affable converse with a young lady. In his voice is the Australian tang that became such a friendly sound to us. He is a rough fellow, sinewy, with the clear eye of the man with the axe whose chief life-struggle till the war came was to fell trees and see to it that they did not crash down on him. Mrs. Otery is showing him the house, which he has evidently known in other days, but though interested he is unsentimental and looks about him with a tolerant grin.

MRS. OTERY. This was the drawing-room.

HARRY. Not it, no, no, never. This wasn't the drawing-room, my cabbage; at least not in my time.

MRS. OTERY (*indifferently*). I only came

here about three years ago and I never saw the house furnished, but I was told to say this was the drawing-room. (*With a flicker of spirit*) And I would thank you not to call me your cabbage.

HARRY (*whom this kind of retort helps to put at his ease*). No offence. It's a French expression, and many a happy moment have I given to the mademoiselles by calling them cabbages. But the drawing-room! I was a little shaver when I was here last, but I mind we called the drawing-room the Big Room; it wasn't a little box like this.

MRS. OTERY. This is the biggest room in the house. (*She quotes drearily from some advertisement which is probably hanging in rags on the gate.*) Specially charming is the drawing-room with its superb view of the Downs. This room is upstairs and is approached by—

HARRY. By a stair, containing some romantic rat-holes. Snakes, whether it's the room or not, it strikes cold; there is something shiversome about it.

(*For the first time she gives him a sharp glance.*)

I've shivered in many a shanty in Australy, and thought of the big room at home and the warmth of it. The warmth! And now this is the best it can do for the prodigal when he returns to it expecting to see that calf done to a turn. We live and learn, missis.

MRS. OTERY. We live, at any rate.

HARRY. Well said, my cabbage.

MRS. OTERY. Thank you, my rhododendron.

HARRY (*cheered*). I like your spirit. You and me would get on great if I had time to devote to your amusement. But, see here, I can make sure whether this was the drawing-room. If it was, there is an apple-tree outside there, with one of its branches scraping on the window. I ought to know, for it was out at the window down that apple-tree to the ground that I slid one dark night when I was a twelve-year-old, ran away from home, the naughty blue-eyed angel that I was, and set off to make my fortune on the blasted ocean. The fortune, my—my lady friend —has still got the start of me, but the apple-tree should be there to welcome her darling boy.

(*He pulls down the sacking, which lets a*

little more light into the room. We see that the window, which reaches to the floor, opens outwards. There were probably long ago steps from it down into the garden, but they are gone now, and gone too is the apple-tree.)

I've won! No tree: no drawing-room.

MRS. OTERY. I have heard tell there was once a tree there; and you can see the root if you look down.

HARRY. Yes, yes, I see it in the long grass, and a bit of the seat that used to be round it. This is the drawing-room right enough, Harry, my boy. There were blue curtains to that window, and I used to hide behind them and pounce out upon Robinson Crusoe. There was a sofa at this end, and I had my first lessons in swimming on it. You are a fortunate woman, my petite, to be here drinking in these moving memories. There used to be a peacock, too. Now, what the hell could a peacock be doing in this noble apartment?

MRS. OTERY. I have been told a cloth used to hang on the wall here, tapestries they're called, and that it had pictures of peacocks on it. I dare say that was your peacock.

HARRY. Gone, even my peacock! And I could have sworn I used to pull the feathers out of its tail. The clock was in this corner, and it had a wheezy little figure of a smith that used to come out and strike the hour on an anvil. My old man used to wind that clock up every night, and I mind his rage when he found out it was an eight-day clock. The padre had to reprove him for swearing. Padre? What's the English for padre? Damme, I'm forgetting my own language. Oh yes, parson. Is *he* in the land of the living still? I can see him clear, a long thin man with a hard sharp face. He was always quarrelling about pictures he collected.

MRS. OTERY. The parson here is a very old man, but he is not tall and thin, he is little and roundish with a soft face and white whiskers.

HARRY. Whiskers? I can't think he had whiskers. (*Ruminating*) *Had* he whiskers? Stop a bit, I believe it is his wife I'm thinking about. I doubt I don't give satisfaction as a sentimental character. Is there any objection, your ladyship, to smoking in the drawing-room ?

MRS. OTERY (*ungraciously*). Smoke if you want.

> (*He hacks into a cake of tobacco with a large clasp knife.*)

That's a fearsome-looking knife.

HARRY. Useful in trench warfare. It's not a knife, it's a visiting-card. You leave it on favoured parties like this.

> (*He casts it at one of the packing-cases, and it sticks quivering in the wood.*)

MRS. OTERY. Were you an officer ?

HARRY. For a few minutes now and again.

MRS. OTERY. You're playing with me.

HARRY. You're so *ir*resistible.

MRS. OTERY. Do you want to see the other rooms ?

HARRY. I was fondly hoping you would ask me that.

MRS. OTERY. Come along then. (*She wants to lead him downstairs, but the little door at the back has caught his eye.*)

HARRY. What does that door open on ?

MRS. OTERY (*avoiding looking at it*). Nothing, it's just a cupboard door.

HARRY (*considering her*). Who is playing with me now?

MRS. OTERY. I don't know what you mean. Come this way.

HARRY (*not budging*). I'll explain what I mean. That door—it's coming back to me—it leads into a little dark passage.

MRS. OTERY. That's all.

HARRY. That can't be all. Who ever heard of a passage wandering about by itself in a respectable house! It leads—yes—to a single room, and the door of the room faces this way.

> (*He opens the door, and a door beyond is disclosed.*)

There's a memory for you! But what the hell made you want to deceive me?

MRS. OTERY. It's of no consequence.

HARRY. I think—yes—the room in there has two stone windows—and wooden rafters.

MRS. OTERY. It's the oldest part of the house.

HARRY. It comes back to me that I used to sleep there.

MRS. OTERY. That may be. If you'll come down with me—

HARRY. I'm curious to see that room first.

(*She bars the way.*)

MRS. OTERY (*thin-lipped and determined*). You can't go in there.

HARRY. Your reasons?

MRS. OTERY. It's—locked. I tell you it's just an empty room.

HARRY. There must be a key.

MRS. OTERY. It's—lost.

HARRY. Queer your anxiety to stop me, when you knew I would find the door locked.

MRS. OTERY. Sometimes it's locked; sometimes not.

HARRY. Is it not you that locks it?

MRS. OTERY (*reluctantly*). It's never locked, it's held.

HARRY. Who holds it?

MRS. OTERY (*in a little outburst*). Quiet, man.

HARRY. You're all shivering.

MRS. OTERY. I'm not.

HARRY (*cunningly*). I suppose you are just shivering because the room is so chilly.

MRS. OTERY (*falling into the trap*). That's it.

HARRY. So you *are* shivering!

> (*She makes no answer, and he reflects with
> the help of his pipe.*)

May I put a light to these bits of sticks?

MRS. OTERY. If you like. My orders are to have fires once a week.

> (*He lights the twigs in the fireplace, and they
> burn up easily, but will be ashes in a few
> minutes.*)

You can't have the money to buy a house like this.

HARRY. Not me. It was just my manly curiosity to see the old home that brought me. I'm for Australy again. (*Suddenly turning on her*) What is wrong with this house?

MRS. OTERY (*on her guard*). There is nothing wrong with it.

HARRY. Then how is it going so cheap?

MRS. OTERY. It's—in bad repair.

HARRY. Why has it stood empty so long?

MRS. OTERY. It's—far from a town.

HARRY. What made the last tenant leave in such a hurry?

MRS. OTERY (*wetting her lips*). You have heard that, have you? Gossiping in the village, I suppose?

HARRY. I have heard some other things as well. I have heard they had to get a caretaker from a distance, because no woman hereabout would live alone in this house.

MRS. OTERY. A pack o' cowards.

HARRY. I have heard that that caretaker was bold and buxom when she came, and that now she is a scared woman.

MRS. OTERY. I'm not.

HARRY. I have heard she's been known to run out into the fields and stay there trembling half the night.

>   (*She does not answer, and he resorts to cunning again.*)

Of course, I see they couldn't have meant you. Just foolish stories that gather about an old house.

MRS. OTERY (*relieved*). That's all.

HARRY (*quickly as he looks at the little door*). What's that?

>   (MRS. OTERY *screams.*)

I got you that time ! What was it you expected to see ?

  (*No answer.*)

Is it a ghost ? They say it's a ghost. What is it gives this house an ill name ?

MRS. OTERY. Use as brave words as you like when you have gone, but I advise you, my lad, to keep a civil tongue while you are here. (*In her everyday voice*) There is no use showing you the rest of the house. If you want to be stepping, I have my work to do.

HARRY. We have got on so nicely, I wonder if you would give me a mug of tea. Not a cup, we drink it by the mugful where I hail from.

MRS. OTERY (*ungraciously*). I have no objection.

HARRY. Since you are so pressing, I accept.

MRS. OTERY. Come down then to the kitchen.

HARRY. No, no, I'm sure the Prodigal got his tea in the drawing-room, though what made them make such a fuss about that man beats me.

MRS. OTERY (*sullenly*). You are meaning to go into that room. I wouldn't if I was you.

HARRY. If you were me you would.

MRS. OTERY (*closing the little door*). Until I have your promise—

HARRY (*liking the tenacity of her*). Very well, I promise—unless, of course, she comes peeping out at the handsome gentleman. Your ghost has naught to do wi' me. It's a woman, isn't it?

(*Her silence is perhaps an assent.*)

See here, I'll sit in this chair till you come back, saying my prayers. (*Feeling the chair*) You're clammy cold, old dear. It's not the ghost's chair by any chance, is it?

(*No answer.*)

You needn't look so scared, woman; she doesn't walk till midnight, does she?

MRS. OTERY (*looking at his knife in the wood*). I wouldn't leave that knife lying about.

HARRY. Oh, come, give the old girl a chance.

MRS. OTERY. I'll not be more than ten minutes.

HARRY. She can't do much in ten minutes.

(*At which remark* MRS. OTERY *fixes him with her eyes and departs.*

HARRY *is now sitting sunk in the chair, staring at the fire. It goes out, but he re-*

mains there motionless, and in the increasing dusk he ceases to be an intruder. He is now part of the room, the part long waited for, come back at last. The house is shaken to its foundation by his presence, we may conceive a thousand whispers. Then the crafty work begins. The little door at the back opens slowly to the extent of a foot. Thus might a breath of wind blow it if there were any wind. Presently HARRY starts to his feet, convinced that there is some one in the room, very near his knife. He is so sure of the exact spot where she is that for a moment he looks nowhere else.

In that moment the door slowly closes. He has not seen it close, but he opens it and calls out, 'Who is that? Is any one there?' With some distaste he enters the passage and tries the inner door, but whether it be locked or held it will not open. He is about to pocket his knife, then with a shrug of bravado sends it quivering back into the wood—for her if she can get it. He returns to the chair, but not to close his eyes; to watch and to be *watched. The room is in a tremble of desire to get started upon that nightly travail which can never be completed till this man is here to provide the end.*

The figure of HARRY *becomes indistinct and fades from sight. When the haze lifts we are looking at the room as it was some thirty years earlier on the serene afternoon that began its troubled story. There are rooms that are always smiling, so that you may see them at it if you peep through the keyhole, and* MRS. MORLAND'S *little drawing-room is one of them. Perhaps these are smiles that she has left lying about. She leaves many things lying about; for instance, one could deduce the shape of her from studying that corner of the sofa which is her favourite seat, and all her garments grow so like her that her wardrobes are full of herself hanging on nails or folded away in drawers. The pictures on her walls in time take on a resemblance to her or hers though they may be meant to represent a waterfall, every present given to her assumes some characteristic of the donor, and no doubt the necktie she is at present knitting will soon be able to pass as the person for whom it is being knit. It is only delightful ladies at the most agreeable age who have this personal way with their belongings. Among* MRS. MORLAND'S *friends in the room are several of whom we have already heard, such as the blue curtains from which* HARRY *pounced upon the castaway, the sofa on which he had his first swimming lessons, the peacock on the wall, the clock with the smart smith ready to step out and strike his anvil, and the apple-tree is in full blossom at the open window, one of its branches has even stepped into the room.*

MR. MORLAND *and the local clergyman are chatting importantly about some matter of no importance, while* MRS. MORLAND *is on her sofa at the other side of the room, coming into the conversation occasionally with a cough or a click of her needles, which is her clandestine way of telling her husband not to be so assertive to his guest. They are all middle-aged people who have found life to be on the whole an easy and happy adventure, and have done their tranquil best to make it so for their neighbours. The squire is lean, the clergyman of full habit, but could you enter into them you would have difficulty in deciding which was clergyman and which was squire; both can be peppery, the same pepper. They are benignant creatures, but could exchange benignancies without altering.* MRS. MORLAND *knows everything about her husband except that she does nearly all his work for him. She really does not know this. His work, though he rises early to be at it, is not much larger than a lady's handkerchief, and consists of magisterial duties, with now and then an impressive scene about a tenant's cowshed. She then makes up his mind for him, and is still unaware that she is doing it. He has so often heard her say (believing it, too) that he is difficult to move when once he puts his foot down that he accepts himself modestly as a man of this character, and never tries to remember when it was that he last put down his foot. In the odd talks which the happily married sometimes hold about the future he always hopes he will be taken first, being the managing one, and she says little beyond pressing his hand, but privately she has decided that there must be another arrangement. Probably life at the vicarage is on not dissimilar lines, but we cannot tell, as we never meet* MR. AMY'S *wife.* MR. AMY *is even more sociable than* MR. MORLAND; *he is reputed to know every one in the county, and has several times fallen off his horse because he will salute all passers-by. On his visits to London he usually returns depressed because there are so many people in the streets to whom he may not give a friendly bow. He likes to read a book if he knows the residence or a relative of the author, and at the play it is far more to him to learn that the actress has three children, one of them down with measles, than to follow her histrionic genius. He and his host have the pleasant habit of print-collecting, and a very common scene between them is that which now follows. They are bent over the squire's latest purchase.)*

MR. AMY. Very interesting. A nice little lot. I must say, James, you have the collector's flare.

MR. MORLAND. Oh, well, I'm keen, you know, and when I run up to London I can't resist going a bust in my small way. I picked these up quite cheap.

MR. AMY. The flare. That is what you have.

MR. MORLAND. Oh, I don't know.

MR. AMY. Yes, you have, James. You got them at Peterkin's in Dean Street, didn't you? Yes, I know you did. I saw them there. I wanted them too, but they told me you had already got the refusal.

MR. MORLAND. Sorry to have been too quick for you, George, but it is my way to nip in. You have some nice prints yourself.

MR. AMY. I haven't got your flare, James.

MR. MORLAND. I admit I don't miss much.

   (*So far it has been a competition in saintliness.*)

MR. AMY. No. (*The saint leaves him.*) You missed something yesterday at Peterkin's though.

MR. MORLAND. How do you mean?

MR. AMY. You didn't examine the little lot lying beneath this lot.

MR. MORLAND. I turned them over; just a few odds and ends of no account.

MR. AMY (*with horrible complacency*). All except one, James.

MR. MORLAND (*twitching*). Something good?

MR. AMY (*at his meekest*). Just a little trifle of a Gainsborough.

MR. MORLAND (*faintly*). What! You've got it?

MR. AMY. I've got it. I am a poor man, but I thought ten pounds wasn't too much for a Gainsborough.

(*The devil now has them both.*)

MR. MORLAND. Ten pounds! Is it signed?

MR. AMY. No, it isn't signed.

MR. MORLAND (*almost his friend again*). Ah!

MR. AMY. What do you precisely mean by that 'Ah,' James? If it had been signed, could I have got it for ten pounds? You are always speaking about your flare; I suppose I can have a little flare sometimes too.

MR. MORLAND. I am not always speaking about my flare, and I don't believe it is a Gainsborough.

MR. AMY (*with dignity*). Please don't get hot, James. If I had thought you would grudge me my little find—which *you* missed—I wouldn't have brought it to show you.

(*With shocking exultation he produces a roll of paper.*)

MR. MORLAND (*backing from it*). So that's it.

MR. AMY. This is it. (*The squire has to examine it like a Christian.*) There! I have the luck this time. I hope you will have it next. (*The exultation now passes from the one face into the other.*)

MR. MORLAND. Interesting, George—quite. But definitely not a Gainsborough.

MR. AMY. I say definitely a Gainsborough.

MR. MORLAND. Definitely not a Gainsborough.

(*By this time the needles have entered*

> *into the controversy, but they are disre-
> garded.*)

I should say the work of a clever amateur.

MR. AMY. Look at the drawing of the cart and the figure beside it.

MR. MORLAND. Weak and laboured. Look at that horse.

MR. AMY. Gainsborough did some very funny horses.

MR. MORLAND. Granted, but he never placed them badly. That horse destroys the whole balance of the composition.

MR. AMY. James, I had no idea you had such a small nature.

MR. MORLAND. I don't like that remark; for your sake I don't like it. No one would have been more pleased than myself if you had picked up a Gainsborough. But this! Besides, look at the paper.

MR. AMY. What is wrong with the paper, Mr. Morland?

MR. MORLAND. It is machine-made. Gainsborough was in his grave years before that paper was made.

> (*After further inspection* MR. AMY *is con-*

*vinced against his will, and the find is
returned to his pocket less carefully than
it had been produced.)*

Don't get into a tantrum about it, George.

MR. AMY (*grandly*). I am not in a tantrum, and I should be obliged if you wouldn't George me. Smile on, Mr. Morland, I congratulate you on your triumph; you have hurt an old friend to the quick. Bravo, bravo. Thank you, Mrs. Morland, for a very pleasant visit. Good-day.

MRS. MORLAND (*prepared*). I shall see you into your coat, George.

MR. AMY. I thank you, Mrs. Morland, but I need no one to see me into my coat. Good-day.

(*He goes, and she blandly follows him. She returns with the culprit.*)

MRS. MORLAND. Now which of you is to say it first?

MR. AMY. James, I am heartily ashamed of myself.

MR. MORLAND. George, I apologise.

MR. AMY. I quite see that it isn't a Gainsborough.

MR. MORLAND. After all, it's certainly in the Gainsborough school.

> (*They clasp hands sheepishly, but the peacemaker helps the situation by showing a roguish face, and* MR. AMY *departs shaking a humorous fist at her.*)

MRS. MORLAND. I coughed so often, James; and you must have heard me clicking.

MR. MORLAND. I heard all right. Good old George! It's a pity he has no flare. He might as well order his prints by wireless.

MRS. MORLAND. What is that?

MR. MORLAND. Wireless it's to be called. There is an article about it in that paper. The fellow says that before many years have passed we shall be able to talk to ships on the ocean.

MRS. MORLAND (*who has resumed her knitting*). Nonsense, James.

MR. MORLAND. Of course it's nonsense. And yet there is no denying, as he says, that there are more things in heaven and earth than are dreamt of in our philosophy.

MRS. MORLAND (*becoming grave*). You and I know that to be true, James.

(*For a moment he does not know to what she is referring.*)

MR. MORLAND (*edging away from trouble*). Oh, that. My dear, that is all dead and done with long ago.

MRS. MORLAND (*thankfully*). Yes. But sometimes when I look at Mary Rose—so happy—

MR. MORLAND. She will never know anything about it.

MRS. MORLAND. No, indeed. But some day she will fall in love—

MR. MORLAND (*wriggling*). That infant! Fanny, is it wise to seek trouble before it comes?

MRS. MORLAND. She can't marry, James, without your first telling the man. We agreed.

MR. MORLAND. Yes, I suppose I must—though I'm not certain I ought to. Sleeping dogs— Still, I'll keep my word, I'll tell him everything.

MRS. MORLAND. Poor Mary Rose.

MR. MORLAND (*manfully*). Now then, none of that. Where is she now?

MRS. MORLAND. Down at the boat-house with Simon, I think.

MR. MORLAND. That is all right. Let her play about with Simon and the like. It may make a tomboy of her, but it will keep young men out of her head.

(*She wonders at his obtuseness.*)

MRS. MORLAND. You still think of Simon as a boy?

MR. MORLAND. Bless the woman, he is only a midshipman.

MRS. MORLAND. A sub-lieutenant now.

MR. MORLAND. Same thing. Why, Fanny, I still tip him. At least I did a year ago. And he liked it: 'Thanks no end, you are a trump,' he said, and then slipped behind the screen to see how much it was.

MRS. MORLAND. He is a very delightful creature; but he isn't a boy any more.

MR. MORLAND. It's not nice of you to put such ideas into my head. I'll go down to the boat-house at once. If this new invention was in working order, Fanny, I could send him packing without rising from my seat. I should simply say from this sofa, 'Is my little Mary Rose there?'

> (*To their surprise there is an answer from* MARY ROSE *unseen.*)

MARY ROSE (*in a voice more quaking than is its wont*). I'm here, Daddy.

MR. MORLAND (*rising*). Where are you, Mary Rose?

MARY ROSE. I am in the apple-tree.

> (MRS. MORLAND *smiles and is going to the window, but her husband checks her with a further exhibition of the marvel of the future.*)

MR. MORLAND. What are you doing in the apple-tree, hoyden?

MARY ROSE. I'm hiding.

MR. MORLAND. From Simon?

MARY ROSE. No; I'm not sure whom I'm hiding from. From myself, I think. Daddy, I'm frightened.

MR. MORLAND. What has frightened you? Simon?

MARY ROSE. Yes—partly.

MR. MORLAND. Who else?

MARY ROSE. I am most afraid of my daddy.

MR. MORLAND (*rather flattered*). Of me?

(*If there is anything strange about this girl of eighteen who steps from the tree into the room, it is an elusiveness of which she is unaware. It has remained hidden from her girl friends, though in the after years, in the brief space before they forget her, they will probably say, because of what happened, that there was always something a little odd about* MARY ROSE. *This oddness might be expressed thus, that the happiness and glee of which she is almost overfull know of another attribute of her that never plays with them.*

There is nothing splendid about MARY ROSE, *never can she become one of those secret women so much less innocent than she, yet perhaps so much sweeter in the kernel, who are the bane or glory, or the bane and glory, of greater lovers than she could ever understand. She is just a rare and lovely flower, far less fitted than those others for the tragic rôle.*

She butts her head into MRS. MORLAND *with a childish impulsiveness that might overthrow a less accustomed bosom.*)

MARY ROSE (*telling everything*). Mother!

MR. MORLAND. You don't mean that anything has really frightened you, Mary Rose?

MARY ROSE. I am not sure. Hold me tight, Mother.

MRS. MORLAND. Darling, has Simon been disturbing you?

MARY ROSE (*liking this way of putting it*). Yes, he has. It is all Simon's fault.

MR. MORLAND. But you said you were afraid even of me.

MARY ROSE. You are the only one.

MR. MORLAND. Is this some game? Where is Simon?

MARY ROSE (*in little mouthfuls*). He is at the foot of the tree. He is not coming up by the tree. He wants to come in by the door. That shows how important it is.

MR. MORLAND. What is?

MARY ROSE. You see, his leave is up to-morrow, and he—wants to see you, Daddy, before he goes.

MR. MORLAND. I am sure he does. And I know why. I told you, Fanny. Mary Rose, do you see my purse lying about?

MARY ROSE. Your purse, Dad?

MR. MORLAND. Yes, you gosling. There is a fiver in it, and *that* is what Master Simon wants to see me about.

(MARY ROSE *again seeks her mother's breast.*)

MRS. MORLAND. Oh, James! Dearest, tell me what Simon has been saying to you; whisper it, my love.

(MARY ROSE *whispers.*)
Yes, I thought it was that.

MARY ROSE. I am frightened to tell Daddy.

MRS. MORLAND. James, you may as well be told bluntly; it isn't your fiver that Simon wants, it is your daughter.

(MR. MORLAND *is aghast, and* MARY ROSE *rushes into his arms to help him in this terrible hour.*)

MARY ROSE (*as the injured party*). You will scold him, won't you, Dad?

MR. MORLAND (*vainly trying to push her from him*). By—by—by the—by all that is horrible I'll do more than scold him. The puppy, I'll—I'll—

MARY ROSE (*entreating*). Not more than scold him, Daddy — not more. Mary Rose couldn't bear it if it was more.

MR. MORLAND (*blankly*). You are not in love with Simon, are you?

MARY ROSE. Oh-h-h-h!

> (*She makes little runnings from the one parent to the other, carrying kisses for the wounds.*)

Daddy, I am so awfully sorry that this has occurred. Mummy, what can we do? (*She cries.*)

MRS. MORLAND (*soothing her*). My own, my pet. But he is only a boy, Mary Rose, just a very nice boy.

MARY ROSE (*awed*). Mother, that is the wonderful, wonderful thing. He was just a boy—I quite understand that—he was a mere

boy till to-day; and then, Daddy, he suddenly
changed; all at once he became a man. It was
while he was—telling me. You will scarcely
know him now, Mother.

MRS. MORLAND. Darling, he breakfasted with
us; I think I shall know him still.

MARY ROSE. He is quite different from
breakfast-time. He doesn't laugh any more,
he would never think of capsizing the punt
intentionally now, he has grown so grave, so
manly, so—so *protective*, he thinks of everything
now, of freeholds and leaseholds, and gravel
soil, and hot and cold, and the hire system.

(*She cries again, but her eyes are sparkling
through the rain.*)

MR. MORLAND (*with spirit*). He has got as
far as that, has he! Does he propose that this
marriage should take place to-morrow?

MARY ROSE (*eager to soften the blow*). Oh no,
not for quite a long time. At earliest, not till
his next leave.

MRS. MORLAND. Mary Rose!

MARY ROSE. He is waiting down there,
Mummy. May I bring him in?

MRS. MORLAND. Of course, dearest.

MR. MORLAND. Don't come with him, though.

MARY ROSE. Oh! (*She wonders what this means.*) You know how shy Simon is.

MR. MORLAND. I do not.

MRS. MORLAND. Your father and I must have a talk with him alone, you see.

MARY ROSE. I—I suppose so. He so wants to do the right thing, Mother.

MRS. MORLAND. I am sure he does.

MARY ROSE. Do you mind my going upstairs into the apple-room and sometimes knocking on the floor? I think it would be a help to him to know I am so near by.

MRS. MORLAND. It would be a help to all of us, my sweet.

MARY ROSE (*plaintively*). You—you won't try to put him against me, Daddy?

MR. MORLAND. I would try my hardest if I thought I had any chance.

> (*When she has gone they are a somewhat forlorn pair.*)

Poor old mother!

MRS. MORLAND. Poor old father! There couldn't be a nicer boy, though.

MR. MORLAND. No, but— (*He has a distressing thought.*)

MRS. MORLAND (*quietly*). Yes, there's that.

MR. MORLAND. It got me on the quick when she said, 'You won't try to put him against me, Daddy'—because that is just what I suppose I have got to do.

MRS. MORLAND. He must be told.

MR. MORLAND (*weakly*). Fanny, let us keep it to ourselves.

MRS. MORLAND. It would not be fair to him.

MR. MORLAND. No, it wouldn't. (*Testily*) He will be an ass if it bothers him.

MRS. MORLAND (*timidly*). Yes.

> (SIMON *comes in, a manly youth of twenty-three in naval uniform. Whether he has changed much since breakfast-time we have no means of determining, but he is sufficiently attractive to make one hope that there will be no further change in the immediate future. He seems younger even than his years, because he is trying to look*

as if a decade or so had passed since the incident of the boat-house and he were now a married man of approved standing. He has come with honeyed words upon his lips, but suddenly finds that he is in the dock. His judges survey him silently, and he can only reply with an idiotic but perhaps ingratiating laugh.)

SIMON. Ha, ha, ha, ha, ha, ha, ha, ha! (*He ceases uncomfortably, like one who has made his statement.*)

MR. MORLAND. You will need to say more than that, you know, Simon, to justify your conduct.

MRS. MORLAND. Oh, Simon, how could you!

SIMON (*with a sinking*). It seems almost like stealing.

MR. MORLAND. It is stealing.

SIMON (*prudently*). Ha, ha, ha, ha, ha, ha!

(*From the ceiling there comes a gentle tapping, as from a senior officer who is indicating that England expects her lieutenant this day to do his duty.* SIMON *inflates.*)

It is beastly hard on you, of course; but if you knew what Mary Rose is!

MRS. MORLAND (*pardonably*). We feel that even we know to some extent what Mary Rose is.

SIMON (*tacking*). Yes, rather; and so you can see how it has come about. (*This effort cheers him.*) I would let myself be cut into little chips for her; I should almost like it. (*With a brief glance at his misspent youth.*) Perhaps you have thought that I was a rather larky sort in the past?

MR. MORLAND (*sarcastically*). We see an extraordinary change in you, Simon.

SIMON (*eagerly*). Have you noticed that? Mary Rose has noticed it too. That is my inner man coming out. (*Carefully*) To some young people marriage is a thing to be entered on lightly, but that is not my style. What I want is to give up larks, and all that, and insure my life, and read the political articles.

(*Further knocking from above reminds him of something else.*)

Yes, and I promise you it won't be like losing a daughter but like gaining a son.

MRS. MORLAND. Did Mary Rose tell you to say that?

SIMON (*guiltily*). Well— (*Tap, tap.*) Oh, another thing, I should consider it well worth being married to Mary Rose just to have you, Mrs. Morland, for a mother-in-law.

MR. MORLAND (*pleased*). Well said, Simon; I like you the better for that.

MRS. MORLAND (*a demon*). Did she tell you to say that also?

SIMON. Well— At any rate, never shall I forget the respect and affection I owe to the parents of my beloved wife.

MR. MORLAND. She is not your wife yet, you know.

SIMON (*handsomely*). No, she isn't. But can she be? Mrs. Morland, can she be?

MRS. MORLAND. That is as may be, Simon. It is only a possible engagement that we are discussing at present.

SIMON. Yes, yes, of course. (*Becoming more difficult to resist as his reason goes.*) I used to be careless about money, but I have thought of a trick of writing the word Economy in the inside of my watch, so that I'll see it every time I wind up. My people—

MR. MORLAND. We like them, Simon.

(*The tapping is resumed.*)

SIMON. I don't know whether you have noticed a sound from up above?

MR. MORLAND. I did think I heard something.

SIMON. That is Mary Rose in the apple-room.

MRS. MORLAND. No!

SIMON. Yes; she is doing that to help me. I promised to knock back as soon as I thought things were going well. What do you say? May I?

(*He gives them an imploring look, and mounts a chair, part of a fishing rod in his hand.*)

MR. MORLAND (*an easy road in sight*). I think, Fanny, he might?

MRS. MORLAND (*braver*). No. (*Tremulously*) There is a little thing, Simon, that Mary Rose's father and I feel we ought to tell you about her before—before you knock, my dear. It is not very important, I think, but it is something she doesn't know of herself, and it makes her a little different from other girls.

SIMON (*alighting—sharply*). I won't believe anything against Mary Rose.

MRS. MORLAND. We have nothing to tell you against her.

MR. MORLAND. It is just something that happened, Simon. She couldn't help it. It hasn't troubled us in the least for years, but we always agreed that she mustn't be engaged before we told the man. We must have your promise, before we tell you, that you will keep it to yourself.

SIMON (*frowning*). I promise.

MRS. MORLAND. You must never speak of it even to her.

SIMON. Not to Mary Rose? I wish you would say quickly what it is.

(*They are now sitting round the little table.*)

MR. MORLAND. It can't be told quite in a word. It happened seven years ago, when Mary Rose was eleven. We were in a remote part of Scotland—in the Outer Hebrides.

SIMON. I once went on shore there from the *Gadfly*, very bleak and barren, rocks and rough grass, I never saw a tree.

MR. MORLAND. It is mostly like that. There is a whaling-station. We went because I was fond of fishing. I haven't had the heart to fish since. Quite close to the inn where we put up there is—a little island.

(*He sees that little island so clearly that he forgets to go on.*)

MRS. MORLAND. It is quite a small island, Simon, uninhabited, no sheep even. I suppose there are only about six acres of it. There are trees there, quite a number of them, Scotch firs and a few rowan-trees,—they have red berries, you know. There seemed to us to be nothing very particular about the island, unless, perhaps, that it is curiously complete in itself. There is a tiny pool in it that might be called a lake, out of which a stream flows. It has hillocks and a glade, a sort of miniature land. That was all we noticed, though it became the most dreaded place in the world to us.

MR. MORLAND (*considerately*). I can tell him without your being here, Fanny.

MRS. MORLAND. I prefer to stay, James.

MR. MORLAND. I fished a great deal in the

loch between that island and the larger one. The sea-trout were wonderful. I often rowed Mary Rose across to the island and left her there to sketch. She was fond of sketching in those days, we thought them pretty things. I could see her from the boat most of the time, and we used to wave to each other. Then I would go back for her when I stopped fishing.

MRS. MORLAND. I didn't often go with them. We didn't know at the time that the natives had a superstition against landing on the island, and that it was supposed to resent this. It had a Gaelic name which means 'The Island that Likes to be Visited.' Mary Rose knew nothing of this, and she was very fond of her island. She used to talk to it, call it her darling, things like that.

SIMON (*restless*). Tell me what happened.

MR. MORLAND. It was on what was to be our last day. I had landed her on this island as usual, and in the early evening I pulled across to take her off. From the boat I saw her, sitting on a stump of a tree that was her favourite seat, and she waved gaily to me and I to her.

Then I rowed over, with, of course, my back to her. I had less than a hundred yards to go, but, Simon, when I got across she wasn't there.

SIMON. You seem so serious about it. She was hiding from you?

MRS. MORLAND. She wasn't on the island, Simon.

SIMON. But—but—oh, but—

MR. MORLAND. Don't you think I searched and searched?

MRS. MORLAND. All of us. No one in the village went to bed that night. It was then we learned how they feared the island.

MR. MORLAND. The little pool was dragged. There was nothing we didn't try; but she was gone.

SIMON (*distressed*). I can't—there couldn't—but never mind that. Tell me how you found her.

MRS. MORLAND. It was the twentieth day after she disappeared. Twenty days!

SIMON. Some boat—?

MR. MORLAND. There was no boat but mine.

SIMON. Tell me.

MRS. MORLAND. The search had long been given up, but we couldn't come away.

MR. MORLAND. I was wandering one day along the shore of the loch, you can imagine in what state of mind. I stopped and stood looking across the water at the island, and, Simon, I saw her sitting on the tree-trunk sketching.

MRS. MORLAND. Mary Rose!

MR. MORLAND. She waved to me and went on sketching. I—I waved back to her. I got into the boat and rowed across just in the old way, except that I sat facing her, so that I could see her all the time. When I landed, the first thing she said to me was, 'Why did you row in that funny way, Dad?' Then I saw at once that she didn't know anything had happened.

SIMON. Mr. Morland! How could—? Where did she say she had been?

MRS. MORLAND. She didn't know she had been anywhere, Simon.

MR. MORLAND. She thought I had just come for her at the usual time.

SIMON. Twenty days. You mean she had been on the island all that time?

MR. MORLAND. We don't know.

MRS. MORLAND. James brought her back to me just the same merry unselfconscious girl, with no idea that she had been away from me for more than an hour or two.

SIMON. But when you told her—

MRS. MORLAND. We never told her; she doesn't know now.

SIMON. Surely you—

MRS. MORLAND. We had her back again, Simon; that was the great thing. At first we thought to tell her after we got her home; and then, it was all so inexplicable, we were afraid to alarm her, to take the bloom off her. In the end we decided never to tell her.

SIMON. You told no one ?

MR. MORLAND. Several doctors.

SIMON. How did they explain it ?

MR. MORLAND. They had no explanation for it except that it never took place. You can think that, too, if you like.

SIMON. I don't know what to think. It has had no effect on her, at any rate.

MR. MORLAND. None whatever—and you can guess how we used to watch.

MRS. MORLAND. Simon, I am very anxious to be honest with you. I have sometimes thought that our girl is curiously young for her age—as if—you know how just a touch of frost may stop the growth of a plant and yet leave it blooming—it has sometimes seemed to me as if a cold finger had once touched my Mary Rose.

SIMON. Mrs. Morland!

MRS. MORLAND. There is nothing in it.

SIMON. What you are worrying about is just her innocence—which seems a holy thing to me.

MRS. MORLAND. And indeed it is.

SIMON. If that is all—

MR. MORLAND. We have sometimes thought that she had momentary glimpses back into that time, but before we could question her in a cautious way about them the gates had closed and she remembered nothing. You never saw her talking to—to some person who wasn't there?

SIMON. No.

MRS. MORLAND. Nor listening, as it were, for some sound that never came?

SIMON. A sound? Do you mean a sound from the island?

MRS. MORLAND. Yes, we think so. But at any rate she has long outgrown those fancies.

(*She fetches a sketch-book from a drawer.*)
Here are the sketches she made. You can take the book away with you and look at them at your leisure.

SIMON. It is a little curious that she has never spoken to me of that holiday. She tells me everything.

MRS. MORLAND. No, that isn't curious, it is just that the island has faded from her memory. I should be troubled if she began to recall it. Well, Simon, we felt we had to tell you. That is all we know, I am sure it is all we shall ever know. What are you going to do?

SIMON. What do you think!

(*He mounts the chair again, and knocks
    triumphantly. A happy tapping replies.*)
You heard? That means it's all right. You'll see how she'll come tearing down to us!

MRS. MORLAND (*kissing him*). You dear boy, you will see how I shall go tearing up to her. (*She goes off.*)

SIMON. I do love Mary Rose, sir.

MR. MORLAND. So do we, Simon. I suppose that made us love her a little more than other daughters are loved. Well, it is dead and done with, and it doesn't disturb me now at all. I hope you won't let it disturb you.

SIMON (*undisturbed*). Rather not. (*Disturbed*) I say, I wonder whether I *have* noticed her listening for a sound?

MR. MORLAND. Not you. We did wisely, didn't we, in not questioning her?

SIMON. Oh, lord, yes. 'The Island that Likes to be Visited.' It is a queer name. (*Boyishly*) I say, let's forget all about it. (*He looks at the ceiling.*) I almost wish her mother hadn't gone up to her. It will make Mary Rose longer in coming down.

MR. MORLAND (*humorous*). Fanny will think of nicer things to say to her than you could think of, Simon.

SIMON. Yes, I know. Ah, now you are

chaffing me. (*Apologetically*) You see, sir, my leave is up to-morrow.

(MARY ROSE *comes rushing in.*)

Mary Rose!

(*She darts past him into her father's arms.*)

MARY ROSE. It isn't you I am thinking of; it is father, it is poor father. Oh, Simon, how could you? Isn't it hateful of him, Daddy!

MR. MORLAND. I should just say it is. Is your mother crying too?

MARY ROSE (*squeaking*). Yes.

MR. MORLAND. I see I am going to have an abominable day. If you two don't mind very much being left alone, I think I'll go up and sit in the apple-room and cry with your mother. It is close and dark and musty up there, and when we feel we can't stick it any longer I'll knock on the floor, Simon, as a sign that we are coming down.

(*He departs on this light note. We see how the minds of these two children match.*)

SIMON. Mary Rose!

MARY ROSE. Oh, Simon—you and me.

SIMON. You and me, that's it. We are *us*, now. Do you like it?

MARY ROSE. It is so fearfully solemn.

SIMON. You are not frightened, are you?

(*She nods.*)

Not at me?

(*She shakes her head.*)

What at?

MARY ROSE. At *it*— Being — married. Simon, after we are married you will sometimes let me play, won't you?

SIMON. Games?

(*She nods.*)

Rather. Why, I'll go on playing rugger myself. Lots of married people play games.

MARY ROSE (*relieved*). I'm glad; Simon, do you love me?

SIMON. Dearest — precious — my life — my sweetheart. Which name do you like best?

MARY ROSE. I'm not sure. They are all very nice. (*She is conscious of the ceiling.*) Oughtn't we to knock to those beloveds to come down?

SIMON. Please don't. I know a lot about old people, darling. I assure you they don't mind very much sitting in dull places.

MARY ROSE. We mustn't be selfish.

SIMON. Honest Injun, it isn't selfishness. You see, I have a ton of things to tell you. About how I put it to them, and how I remembered what you told me to say, and the way I got the soft side of them. They have heard it all already, so it would really be selfish to bring them down.

MARY ROSE. I'm not so sure.

SIMON. I'll tell you what we'll do. Let's go back to the boat-house, and then they can come down and be cosy here.

MARY ROSE (*gleeful*). Let's! We can stay there till tea-time. (*She wants to whirl him away at once.*)

SIMON. It is fresh down there; put on a jacket, my star.

MARY ROSE. Oh, bother!

SIMON (*firmly*). My child, you are in my care now; I am responsible for you, and I order you to put on a jacket.

MARY ROSE. Order! Simon, you do say the loveliest things. I'll put it on at once.

(*She is going towards the little door at the back, but turns to say something important.*)
Simon, I'll tell you a funny thing about me.

I may be wrong, but I think I'll sometimes love you to kiss me, and sometimes it will be better not.

SIMON. All right. Tell me, what were you thinking as you sat up there in the apple-room, waiting?

MARY ROSE. Holy things.

SIMON. About love?

(*She nods.*)

MARY ROSE. We'll try to be good, won't we, Simon, please?

SIMON. Rather. Honest Injun, we'll be nailers. Did you think of—our wedding-day?

MARY ROSE. A little.

SIMON. Only a little?

MARY ROSE. But frightfully clearly. (*Suddenly*) Simon, I had such a delicious idea about our honeymoon. There is a place in Scotland—in the Hebrides—I should love to go there.

SIMON (*taken aback*). The Hebrides?

MARY ROSE. We once went to it when I was little. Isn't it funny, I had almost forgotten about that island, and then suddenly I saw it quite clearly as I was sitting up there. (*Sense-*

lessly) Of course it was the little old woman who pointed it out to me.

(SIMON *is disturbed*.)

SIMON (*gently*). Mary Rose, there are only yourselves and the three maids in the house, aren't there?

MARY ROSE (*surprised*). You know there are. Whatever makes you ask?

SIMON (*cautiously*). I thought—I thought I had a glimpse of a little old woman on the stair to-day.

MARY ROSE (*interested*). Who on earth could that be?

SIMON. It doesn't matter, I had made a mistake. Tell me, what was there particular about that place in the Hebrides?

MARY ROSE. Oh, the fishing for father. But there was an island where I often— My little island!

SIMON (*perhaps quite unnecessarily*). What are you listening for, Mary Rose?

MARY ROSE. Was I? I don't hear anything. Oh, my dear, my dear, I should love to show you the tree-trunk and the rowan-tree where I used to sketch while father was in the boat. I expect he used to land me on the island because it was such a safe place.

SIMON (*troubled*). That had been the idea. I am not going to spend my honeymoon by the sea, though. And yet I should like to go to the Hebrides—some day—to see that island.

MARY ROSE. Yes, let's.

(*She darts off through the little door for her jacket.*)

ACT II

ACT II

An island in the Outer Hebrides. A hundred yards away, across the loch at the back, may be seen the greater island of which this might be but a stone cast into the sea by some giant hand: perhaps an evil stone which the big island had to spew forth but could not sink. It is fair to look upon to-day, all its menace hidden under mosses of various hues that are a bath to the eye; an island placid as a cow grazing or a sulky lady asleep. The sun which has left the bleak hills beyond is playing hide and seek on it—one suddenly has the curious fancy to ask, with whom? A blessed spot it might be thought, rather than sinister, were there not those two trees, a fir and a rowan, their arms outstretched for ever southward, as if they had been struck while in full flight and could no longer pray to their gods to carry them away from this island. A young Highlander, a Cameron, passes in a boat at the back. MARY ROSE *and* SIMON *come into view on the island. We have already heard them swishing a way through whins and bracken that are unseen. They are dressed as English people dress in Scotland.*

They have been married for four years and are still the gay young creatures of their engagement day. Their talk is the happy nonsense that leaves no ripple unless the unexpected happens.

MARY ROSE (*thrilled*). I think, I think, I don't think at all, I am quite sure. This is the place. Simon, kiss me, kiss me quick. You promised to kiss me quick when we found the place.

SIMON (*obeying*). I am not the man to break my word. At the same time, Mary Rose, I would point out to you that this is the third spot you have picked out as being the place, and three times have I kissed you quick on that understanding. This can't go on, you know. As for your wonderful island, it turns out to be about the size of the Round Pond.

MARY ROSE. I always said it was little like myself.

SIMON. It was obviously made to fit you, or you to fit it; one of you was measured for the other. At any rate, we have now been all round it, and all through it, as my bleeding limbs testify. (*The whins have been tearing at him, and he rubs his legs.*)

MARY ROSE. They didn't hurt me at all.

SIMON. Perhaps they like you better than me. Well, we have made a good search for the place where you used to sit and sketch, and you must now take your choice.

MARY ROSE. It was here. I told you of the fir and the rowan-tree.

SIMON. There were a fir and a rowan at each of the other places.

MARY ROSE. Not this fir, not this rowan.

SIMON. You have me there.

MARY ROSE. Simon, I know I'm not clever, but I'm always right. The rowan-berries! I used to put them in my hair. (*She puts them in her hair again.*) Darling rowan-tree, are you glad to see me back? You don't look a bit older, how do you think *I* am wearing? I shall tell you a secret. You too, firry. Come closer, both of you. Put your arms around me, and listen: I am married!

(*The branch of which she has been making a scarf disengages itself.*)

It didn't like that, Simon, it is jealous. After

all, it knew me first. Dearest trees, if I had known that you felt for me in that way—but it is too late now. I have been married for nearly four years, and this is the man. His name is Lieutenant Simon Sobersides. (*She darts about making discoveries.*)

SIMON (*tranquilly smoking*). What is it now?

MARY ROSE. That moss! I feel sure there is a tree-trunk beneath it, the very root on which I used to sit and sketch.

(*He clears away some of the moss.*)

SIMON. It is a tree-trunk right enough.

MARY ROSE. I believe—I believe I cut my name on it with a knife.

SIMON. This looks like it. 'M—A—R—' and there it stops. That is always where the blade of the knife breaks.

MARY ROSE. My ownest seat, how I have missed you.

SIMON. Don't you believe it, old tree-trunk. She had forgotten all about you, and you just came vaguely back to her mind because we happened to be in the neighbourhood.

MARY ROSE. Yes, I suppose that is true. You were the one who wanted to come, Simon. I wonder why?

SIMON (*with his answer ready*). No particular reason. I wanted to see a place you had visited as a child; that was all. But what a trumpery island it proves to be.

MARY ROSE (*who perhaps agrees with him*). How can you? Even if it is true, you needn't say it before them all, hurting their feelings. Dear seat, here is one for each year I have been away. (*She kisses the trunk a number of times.*)

SIMON (*counting*). Eleven. Go on, give it all the news. Tell it we don't have a house of our own yet.

MARY ROSE. You see, dear seat, we live with my daddy and mother, because Simon is so often away at sea. You know, the loveliest thing in the world is the navy, and the loveliest thing in the navy is H.M.S. *Valiant*, and the loveliest thing on H.M.S. *Valiant* is Lieutenant Simon Sobersides, and the loveliest thing on Lieutenant Simon Sobersides is the little tuft of hair which will keep standing up at the back of his head.

>   (SIMON, *who is lolling on the moss, is so used to her prattle that his eyes close.*)

But, listen, you trees, I have a much more wonderful secret than that. You can have three guesses. It is this . . . I—have—got—a baby! A girl? No thank you. He is two years and nine months, and he says such beautiful things to me about loving me. Oh, rowan, do you think he means them?

SIMON. I distinctly heard it say yes.

>   (*He opens his eyes, to see her gazing entranced across the water.*)

You needn't pretend that you can see him.

MARY ROSE. I do. Can't you? He is waving his bib to us.

SIMON. That is nurse's cap.

MARY ROSE. Then he is waving it. How clever of him. (*She waves her handkerchief.*) Now they are gone. Isn't it funny to think that from this very spot I used to wave to father? That was a happy time.

SIMON. I should be happier here if I wasn't

so hungry. I wonder where Cameron is. I told him after he landed us to tie up the boat at any good place and make a fire. I suppose I had better try to make it myself.

MARY ROSE. How you can think of food at such a time!

SIMON (*who is collecting sticks*). All very well, but you will presently be eating more than your share.

MARY ROSE. Do you know, Simon, I don't think daddy and mother like this island.

SIMON (*on his guard*). Help me with the fire, you chatterbox.

> (*He has long ceased to credit the story he heard four years ago, but he is ever watchful for* MARY ROSE.)

MARY ROSE. They never seem to want to speak of it.

SIMON. Forgotten it, I suppose.

MARY ROSE. I shall write to them from the inn this evening. How surprised they will be to know I am there again.

SIMON (*casually*). I wouldn't write from there. Wait till we cross to the mainland.

MARY ROSE. Why not from there?

SIMON. Oh, no reason. But if they have a distaste for the place, perhaps they wouldn't like our coming. I say, praise me, I have got this fire alight.

MARY ROSE (*who is occasionally pertinacious*). Simon, why did you want to come to my island without me?

SIMON. Did I? Oh, I merely suggested your remaining at the inn because I thought you seemed tired. I wonder where Cameron can have got to.

MARY ROSE. Here he comes. (*Solicitously*) Do be polite to him, dear; you know how touchy they are.

SIMON. I am learning!

> (*The boat, with* CAMERON, *draws in. He is a gawky youth of twenty, in the poor but honourable garb of the ghillie, and is not specially impressive until you question him about the universe.*)

CAMERON (*in the soft voice of the Highlander*). Iss it the wish of Mr. Blake that I should land?

SIMON. Yes. yes, Cameron, with the luncheon.

(CAMERON *steps ashore with a fishing basket.*)

CAMERON. Iss it the wish of Mr. Blake that I open the basket?

SIMON. We shall tumble out the luncheon if you bring a trout or two. I want you to show my wife, Cameron, how one cooks fish by the water's edge.

CAMERON. I will do it with pleasure. (*He pauses.*) There iss one little matter; it iss of small importance. You may haf noticed that I always address you as Mr. Blake. I notice that you always address me as Cameron; I take no offence.

MARY ROSE. Oh dear, I am sure I always address you as Mr. Cameron.

CAMERON. That iss so, ma'am. You may haf noticed that I always address you as 'ma'am.' It iss my way of indicating that I consider you a ferry genteel young matron, and of all such I am the humble servant. (*He pauses.*) In saying I am your humble servant I do not imply that I am not as good as you are. With this brief explanation, ma'am, I will now fetch the trouts.

SIMON (*taking advantage of his departure*). That is one in the eye for me. But I'm hanged if I mister him.

MARY ROSE. Simon, do be careful. If you want to say anything to me that is dangerous, say it in French.

(CAMERON *returns with two small sea-trout.*)

CAMERON. The trouts, ma'am, having been cleaned in a thorough and yet easy manner by pulling them up and down in the water, the next procedure iss as follows.

(*He wraps up the trout in a piece of newspaper and soaks them in the water.*)

I now place the soaking little parcels on the fire, and when the paper begins to burn it will be a sure sign that the trouts iss now ready, like myself, ma'am, to be your humble servants. (*He is returning to the boat.*)

MARY ROSE (*who has been preparing the feast*). Don't go away.

CAMERON. If it iss agreeable to Mistress Blake I would wish to go back to the boat.

MARY ROSE. Why?

(CAMERON *is not comfortable.*)

It would be more agreeable to me if you would stay.

CAMERON (*shuffling*). I will stay.

SIMON. Good man—and look after the trout. It is the most heavenly way of cooking fish, Mary Rose.

CAMERON. It iss a tasty way, Mr. Blake, but I would not use the word heavenly in this connection.

SIMON. I stand corrected. (*Tartly*) I must say—

MARY ROSE. *Prenez garde, mon brave!*

SIMON. *Mon Dieu! Qu'il est un drôle!*

MARY ROSE. *Mais moi, je l'aime; il est tellement—* What is the French for an original?

SIMON. That stumps me.

CAMERON. Colloquially *coquin* might be used, though the classic writers would probably say simply *un original*.

SIMON (*with a groan*). Phew, this is serious. What was that book you were reading, Cameron, while I was fishing?

CAMERON. It iss a small Euripides I carry in the pocket, Mr. Blake.

SIMON. Latin, Mary Rose!

CAMERON. It may be Latin, but in these parts we know no better than to call it Greek.

SIMON. Crushed again! But I dare say it is good for me. Sit down and have pot-luck with us.

CAMERON. I thank you, Mr. Blake, but it would not be good manners for a paid man to sit with his employers.

MARY ROSE. When I ask you, Mr. Cameron?

CAMERON. It iss kindly meant, but I haf not been introduced to you.

MARY ROSE. Oh, but—oh, do let me. My husband Mr. Blake—Mr. Cameron.

CAMERON. I hope you are ferry well, sir.

SIMON. The same to you, Mr. Cameron. How do you do? Lovely day, isn't it?

CAMERON. It iss a fairly fine day. (*He is not yet appeased.*)

MARY ROSE (*to the rescue*). Simon!

SIMON. Ah! Do you know my wife? Mr. Cameron—Mrs. Blake.

CAMERON. I am ferry pleased to make Mistress Blake's acquaintance. Iss Mistress Blake making a long stay in these parts?

MARY ROSE. No, alas, we go across to-morrow.

CAMERON. I hope the weather will be favourable.

MARY ROSE. Thank you (*passing him the sandwiches*). And now, you know, you are our guest.

CAMERON. I am much obliged. (*He examines the sandwiches with curiosity.*) Butcher-meat! This iss ferry excellent.

(*He bursts into a surprising fit of laughter, and suddenly cuts it off.*)

Please to excuse my behaviour. You haf been laughing at me all this time, but you did not know I haf been laughing at myself also, though keeping a remarkable control over my features. I will now haf my laugh out, and then I will explain. (*He finishes his laugh.*) I will now explain. I am not the solemn prig I haf pretended to you to be, I am really a fairly attractive young man, but I am shy and I haf been guarding against your taking liberties with me, not because of myself, who am nothing, but because of the noble profession it iss my ambition to enter. (*They discover that they like him.*)

MARY ROSE. Do tell us what that is.

CAMERON. It iss the ministry. I am a student of Aberdeen University, and in the vacation I am a boatman, or a ghillie, or anything you please, to help to pay my fees.

SIMON. Well done!

CAMERON. I am obliged to Mr. Blake. And I may say, now that we know one another socially, that there iss much in Mr. Blake which I am trying to copy.

SIMON. Something in me worth copying!

CAMERON. It iss not Mr. Blake's learning; he has not much learning, but I haf always understood that the English manage without it. What I admire in you iss your ferry nice manners and your general deportment, in all which I haf a great deal to learn yet, and I watch these things in Mr. Blake and take memoranda of them in a little note-book.

(SIMON *expands.*)

MARY ROSE. Mr. Cameron, do tell me that I also am in the little note-book?

CAMERON. You are not, ma'am, it would not be seemly in me. But it iss written in my heart, and also I haf said it to my father, that I will remain a bachelor unless I can marry some lady who iss ferry like Mistress Blake.

MARY ROSE. Simon, you never said anything to me as pretty as that. Is your father a crofter in the village?

CAMERON. Yes, ma'am, when he iss not at the University of Aberdeen.

SIMON. My stars, does he go there too?

CAMERON. He does so. We share a ferry small room between us.

SIMON. Father and son. Is he going into the ministry also?

CAMERON. Such iss not his purpose. When he has taken his degree he will return and be a crofter again.

SIMON. In that case I don't see what he is getting out of it.

CAMERON. He iss getting the grandest thing in the world out of it; he iss getting education.

(SIMON *feels that he is being gradually rubbed out, and it is a relief to him that*

CAMERON *has now to attend to the trout. The paper they are wrapped in has begun to burn.*)

MARY ROSE (*for the first time eating of trout as it should be cooked*). Delicious! (*She offers a portion to* CAMERON.)

CAMERON. No, I thank you. I haf lived on trouts most of my life. This butcher-meat iss more of an excellent novelty to me.

(*He has been standing all this time.*)

MARY ROSE. Do sit down, Mr. Cameron.

CAMERON. I am doing ferry well here, I thank you.

MARY ROSE. But, please.

CAMERON (*with decision*). I will not sit down on this island.

SIMON (*curiously*). Come, come, are you superstitious, you who are going into the ministry?

CAMERON. This island has a bad name. I haf never landed on it before.

MARY ROSE. A bad name, Mr. Cameron? Oh, but what a shame! When I was here long ago, I often came to the island.

CAMERON. Iss that so? It was not a chancey thing to do.

MARY ROSE. But it is a darling island.

CAMERON. That iss the proper way to speak of it.

MARY ROSE. I am sure I never heard a word against it. Have you, Simon?

SIMON (*brazenly*). Not I. I have heard that its Gaelic name has an odd meaning—'The Island that Likes to be Visited,' but there is nothing terrifying in that.

MARY ROSE. The name is new to me, Mr. Cameron. I think it is sweet.

CAMERON. That iss as it may be, Mistress Blake.

SIMON. What is there against the island?

CAMERON. For one thing, they are saying it has no authority to be here. It was not always here, so they are saying. Then one day it was here.

SIMON. That little incident happened before your time, I should say, Mr. Cameron.

CAMERON. It happened before the time of any one now alive, Mr. Blake.

SIMON. I thought so. And does the island ever go away for a jaunt in the same way?

CAMERON. There are some who say that it does.

SIMON. But you have not seen it on the move yourself?

CAMERON. I am not always watching it, Mr. Blake.

SIMON. Anything else against it?

CAMERON. There iss the birds. Too many birds come here. The birds like this island more than iss seemly.

SIMON. Birds here! What could bring them here?

CAMERON. It iss said they come to listen.

SIMON. To listen to the silence? An island that is as still as an empty church.

CAMERON. I do not know; that iss what they say.

MARY ROSE. I think it is a lovely story about the birds. I expect the kind things come because this island likes to be visited.

CAMERON. That iss another thing; for, mark you, Mistress Blake, an island that had visitors would not need to want to be visited. And why has it not visitors? Because they are afraid to visit it.

MARY ROSE. Whatever are they afraid of?

CAMERON. That iss what I say to them. Whateffer are you afraid of, I say.

MARY ROSE. But what are *you* afraid of, Mr. Cameron?

CAMERON. The same thing that they are afraid of. There are stories, ma'am.

MARY ROSE. Do tell us. Simon, wouldn't it be lovely if he would tell us some misty, eerie Highland stories?

SIMON. I don't know; not unless they are pretty ones.

MARY ROSE. Please, Mr. Cameron! I love to have my blood curdled.

CAMERON. There iss many stories. There iss that one of the boy who was brought to this island. He was no older than your baby.

SIMON. What happened to him?

CAMERON. No one knows, Mr. Blake. His father and mother and their friends, they were gathering rowans on the island, and when they looked round he was gone.

SIMON. Lost?

CAMERON. He could not be found. He was never found.

MARY ROSE. Never! He had fallen into the water?

CAMERON. That iss a good thing to say, that he had fallen into the water. That iss what I say.

SIMON. But you don't believe it?

CAMERON. I do not.

MARY ROSE. What do the people in the village say?

CAMERON. Some say he iss on the island still.

SIMON. Mr. Cameron! Oh, Mr. Cameron! What does your father say?

CAMERON. He will be saying that they are not here always, but that they come and go.

SIMON. They? Who are they?

CAMERON (*uncomfortably*). I do not know.

SIMON. Perhaps he heard what the birds come to listen to!

CAMERON. That iss what they say. He had heard the island calling.

SIMON (*hesitating*). How does the island call?

CAMERON. I do not know.

SIMON. Do you know any one who has heard the call?

CAMERON. I do not. No one can hear it but those for whom it iss meant.

MARY ROSE. But if that child heard it, the others must have heard it also, as they were with him.

CAMERON. They heard nothing. This iss how it will be. I might be standing close to you, Mistress Blake, as it were here, and I might hear it, ferry loud, terrible, or in soft whispers— no one knows—but I would haf to go, and you will not haf heard a sound.

MARY ROSE. Simon, isn't it creepy!

SIMON. But full of holes, I have no doubt. How long ago is this supposed to have happened, credulous one?

CAMERON. It was before I was born.

SIMON. I thought so.

MARY ROSE. Simon, don't make fun of my island. Do you know any more ducky stories about it, Mr. Cameron?

CAMERON. I cannot tell them if Mr. Blake will be saying things the island might not like to hear.

SIMON. Not 'chancey,' I suppose.

MARY ROSE. Simon, promise to be good.

SIMON. All right, Cameron.

CAMERON. This one iss about a young English miss, and they say she was about ten years of age.

MARY ROSE. Not so much younger than I was when I came here. How long ago was it?

CAMERON. I think it iss ten years ago this summer.

MARY ROSE. Simon, it must have been the year after I was here!

(SIMON *thinks she has heard enough.*)

SIMON. Very likely. But, I say, we mustn't stay on gossiping. We must be getting back. Did you bail out the boat?

CAMERON. I did not, but I will do it now if such iss your wish.

MARY ROSE. The story first; I won't go without the story.

CAMERON. Well, then, the father of this miss

he will be fond of the fishing, and he sometimes landed the little one on the island while he fished round it from the boat.

MARY ROSE. Just as father used to do with me!

SIMON. I dare say lots of bold tourists come over here.

CAMERON. That iss so, if ignorance be boldness, and sometimes—

SIMON. Quite so. But I really think we must be starting.

MARY ROSE. No, dear. Please go on, Mr. Cameron.

CAMERON. One day the father pulled over for his little one as usual. He saw her from the boat, and it iss said she kissed her hand to him. Then in a moment more he reached the island, but she was gone.

MARY ROSE. Gone?

CAMERON. She had heard the call of the island, though no sound came to him.

MARY ROSE. Doesn't it make one shiver!

CAMERON. My father was one of the searchers; for many days they searched.

MARY ROSE. But it would not take many minutes to search this darling little island.

CAMERON. They searched, ma'am, long after there was no sense in searching.

MARY ROSE. What a curdling story! Simon dear, it might have been Mary Rose. Is there any more?

CAMERON. There iss more. It was about a month afterwards. Her father was walking on the shore, over there, and he saw something moving on the island. All in a tremble, ma'am, he came across in the boat, and it was his little miss.

MARY ROSE. Alive?

CAMERON. Yes, ma'am.

MARY ROSE. I am glad: but it rather spoils the mystery.

SIMON. How, Mary Rose?

MARY ROSE. Because she could tell them what happened, stupid. Whatever was it?

CAMERON. It iss not so easy as that. She did not know that anything had happened. She thought she had been parted from her father for but an hour.

(MARY ROSE *shivers and takes her husband's hand.*)

SIMON (*speaking more lightly than he is feeling*). You and your bogies and wraiths, you man of the mists.

MARY ROSE (*smiling*). Don't be alarmed, Simon; I was only pretending.

CAMERON. It iss not good to disbelieve the stories when you are in these parts. I believe them all when I am here, though I turn the cold light of remorseless Reason on them when I am in Aberdeen.

SIMON. Is that 'chancey,' my friend? An island that has such extraordinary powers could surely send its call to Aberdeen or farther.

CAMERON (*troubled*). I had not thought of that. That may be ferry true.

SIMON. Beware, Mr. Cameron, lest some day when you are preaching far from here the call plucks you out of the very pulpit and brings you back to the island like a trout on a long cast.

CAMERON. I do not like Mr. Blake's way of talking. I will go and bail the boat.

> (*He goes back to the boat, which soon drifts out of sight.*)

MARY ROSE (*pleasantly thrilled*). Suppose it were true, Simon!

SIMON (*stoutly*). But it isn't.

MARY ROSE. No, of course not; but if it had been, how awful for the girl when her father told her that she had been away for weeks.

SIMON. Perhaps she was never told. He may have thought it wiser not to disturb her.

MARY ROSE. Poor girl! Yes, I suppose that would have been best. And yet—it was taking a risk.

SIMON. How?

MARY ROSE. Well, not knowing what had happened before, she might come back and—and be caught again. (*She draws closer to him.*) Little island, I don't think I like you to-day.

SIMON. If she ever comes back, let us hope it is with an able-bodied husband to protect her.

MARY ROSE (*comfortably*). Nice people, husbands. You won't let them catch me, will you, Simon?

SIMON. Let 'em try. (*Gaily*) And now to pack up the remnants of the feast and escape from the scene of the crime. We will never come back again, Mary Rose, I'm too frightened!

(*She helps him to pack.*)

MARY ROSE. It is a shame to be funny about my island. You poor, lonely isle. I never knew about your liking to be visited, and I dare say I shall never visit you any more. The last time of anything is always sad, don't you think, Simon?

SIMON (*briskly*). There must always be a last time, dearest dear.

MARY ROSE. Yes—I suppose—for everything. There must be a last time I shall see you, Simon. (*Playing with his hair*) Some day I shall flatten this tuft for the thousandth time, and then never do it again.

SIMON. Some day I shall look for it and it won't be there. That day I shall say 'Good riddance.'

MARY ROSE. I shall cry. (*She is whimsical rather than merry and merry rather than sad.*)

(SIMON *touches her hair with his lips.*)
Some day, Simon, you will kiss me for the last time.

SIMON. That wasn't the last time, at any rate. (*To prove it he kisses her again, sportively, little thinking that this may be the last time. She quivers.*) What is it?

MARY ROSE. I don't know; something seemed to pass over me.

SIMON. You and your last times. Let me tell you, Mistress Blake, there will be a last time of seeing your baby. (*Hurriedly*) I mean only that he can't always be infantile; but the day after you have seen him for the last time as a baby you will see him for the first time as a little gentleman. Think of that.

MARY ROSE (*clapping her hands*). The loveliest time of all will be when he is a man and takes me on his knee instead of my putting him on mine. Oh, gorgeous! (*With one of her sudden changes*) Don't you think the sad thing is that

we seldom know when the last time has come?
We could make so much more of it.

SIMON. Don't you believe that. To know
would spoil it all.

(*The packing is nearly completed.*)
I suppose I ought to stamp out the fire?

MARY ROSE. Let Cameron do that. I want
you to come and sit beside me, Simon, and make
love to me.

SIMON. What a life. Let me see now, how
does one begin? Which arm is it? I believe
I have forgotten the way.

MARY ROSE. Then I shall make love to you.
(*Playing with his hair*) Have I been a nice wife
to you, Simon? I don't mean always and
always. There was that awful day when I
threw the butter-dish at you. I am so sorry.
But have I been a tolerably good wife on the
whole, not a wonderful one, but a wife that
would pass in a crowd?

SIMON. Look here, if you are going to butt
me with your head in that way, you must take
that pin out of your hair.

MARY ROSE. Have I been all right as a

mother, Simon? Have I been the sort of mother a child could both love and respect?

SIMON. That is a very awkward question. You must ask that of Harry Morland Blake.

MARY ROSE. Have I— ?

SIMON. Shut up, Mary Rose. I know you: you will be crying in a moment, and you don't have a handkerchief, for I wrapped it round the trout whose head came off.

MARY ROSE. At any rate, Simon Blake, say you forgive me about the butter-dish.

SIMON. I am not so sure of that.

MARY ROSE. And there were some other things—almost worse than the butter-dish.

SIMON. I should just say there were.

MARY ROSE. Simon, how can you? There was nothing so bad as that.

SIMON (*shaking his head*). I can smile at it now, but at the time I was a miserable man. I wonder I didn't take to drink.

MARY ROSE. Poor old Simon. But how stupid you were, dear, not to understand.

SIMON. How could an ignorant young husband understand that it was a good sign when his wife threw the butter-dish at him?

MARY ROSE. You should have guessed.

SIMON. No doubt I was a ninny. But I had always understood that when a young wife— that then she took the husband aside and went red, or white, and hid her head on his bosom, and whispered the rest. I admit I was hoping for that; but all I got was the butter-dish.

MARY ROSE. I suppose different women have different ways.

SIMON. I hope so. (*Severely*) And that was a dastard trick you played me afterwards.

MARY ROSE. Which? Oh, that! I just wanted you to be out of the way till all was over.

SIMON. I don't mean your getting me out of the house, sending me to Plymouth. The dastardliness was in not letting them tell me, when I got back, that—that he had arrived.

MARY ROSE. It was very naughty of me. You remember, Simon, when you came in to my room you tried to comfort me by saying it wouldn't be long now—and I let you maunder on, you darling.

SIMON. Gazing at me with solemn, innocent eyes. You unutterable brat, Mary Rose!

MARY ROSE. You should have been able to read in my face how clever I had been. Oh, Simon, when I said at last, 'Dearest, what is that funny thing in the bassinette?' and you went and looked, never shall I forget your face.

SIMON. I thought at first it was some baby you had borrowed.

MARY ROSE. I sometimes think so still. I didn't, did I?

SIMON. You are a droll one. Always just when I think I know you at last I have to begin at the beginning again.

MARY ROSE (*suddenly*). Simon, if one of us had to—to go—and we could choose which one—

SIMON (*sighing*). She's off again.

MARY ROSE. Well, but if—I wonder which would be best. I mean for Harry, of course.

SIMON. Oh, I should have to hop it.

MARY ROSE. Dear!

SIMON. Oh, I haven't popped off yet. Steady, you nearly knocked over the pickles. (*He regards her curiously.*) If I did go, I know your first thought would be ' The happiness of Harry must not be interfered with for a moment.' You would blot me out for ever, Mary Rose, rather than he should lose one of his hundred laughs a day.

(*She hides her face.*)

It's true, isn't it?

MARY ROSE. It is true, at any rate, that if I was the one to go, that is what I should like you to do.

SIMON. Get off the table-cloth.

(*Her mouth opens.*)

Don't step on the marmalade.

MARY ROSE (*gloriously*). Simon, isn't life lovely! I am so happy, happy, happy. Aren't you?

SIMON. Rather.

MARY ROSE. But you can tie up marmalade. Why don't you scream with happiness? One of us has got to scream.

SIMON. Then I know which one it will be. Scream away, it will give Cameron the jumps.

(CAMERON *draws in.*)

There you are, Cameron. We are still safe, you see. You can count us—two.

CAMERON. I am ferry glad.

SIMON. Here you are (*handing him the luncheon basket*). You needn't tie the boat up. Stay there and I'll stamp out the fire myself.

CAMERON. As Mr. Blake pleases.

SIMON. Ready, Mary Rose?

MARY ROSE. I must say good-bye to my island first. Good-bye, old mossy seat, nice rowan. Good-bye, little island that likes too much to be visited. Perhaps I shall come back when I am an old lady with wrinkles, and you won't know your Mary Rose.

SIMON. I say, dear, do dry up. I can't help listening to you when I ought to be getting this fire out.

MARY ROSE. I won't say another word.

SIMON. Just as it seems to be out, sparks come again. Do you think if I were to get some stones— ?

> (*He looks up and she signs that she has promised not to talk. They laugh to each other. He is then occupied for a little time in dumping wet stones from the loch upon the fire.* CAMERON *is in the boat with his*

Euripides. MARY ROSE *is sitting demure but gay, holding her tongue with her fingers like a child.*

Something else is happening; the call has come to MARY ROSE. *It is at first as soft and furtive as whisperings from holes in the ground, Mary Rose, Mary Rose. Then in a fury as of storm and whistling winds that might be an unholy organ it rushes upon the island, raking every bush for her. These sounds increase rapidly in volume till the mere loudness of them is horrible. They are not without an opponent. Struggling through them, and also calling her name, is to be heard music of an unearthly sweetness that is seeking perhaps to beat them back and put a girdle of safety round her. Once* MARY ROSE'S *arms go out to her husband for help, but thereafter she is oblivious of his existence. Her face is rapt, but there is neither fear nor joy in it. Thus she passes from view. The island immediately resumes its stillness. The sun has gone down.* SIMON *by the fire and* CAMERON *in the boat have heard nothing.*)

SIMON (*on his knees*). I think the fire is done for at last, and that we can go now. How cold and grey it has become. (*Smiling, but without looking up*) You needn't grip your tongue any longer, you know. (*He rises.*) Mary Rose, where have you got to? Please don't hide. Dearest, don't. Cameron, where is my wife?

(CAMERON *rises in the boat, and he is afraid to land. His face alarms* SIMON, *who runs this way and that and is lost to sight calling her by name again and again. He returns livid.*)

Cameron, I can't find her. Mary Rose! Mary Rose! Mary Rose!

ACT III

ACT III

Twenty-five years have passed, and the scene is again that cosy room in the Morlands' house, not much changed since we last saw it. If chintzes have faded, others as smiling have taken their place. The time is a crisp autumn afternoon just before twilight comes. The apple-tree, not so easy to renew as the chintzes, has become smaller, but there are a few gallant apples on it. The fire is burning, and round it sit Mr. and Mrs. Morland and Mr. Amy, the Morlands gone smaller like the apple-tree and Mr. Amy bulky, but all three on the whole still bearing their apples. Inwardly they have changed still less; hear them at it as of yore.

MR. MORLAND. What are you laughing over, Fanny?

MRS. MORLAND. It is this week's *Punch*, so very amusing.

MR. AMY. Ah, *Punch*, it isn't what it used to be.

MR. MORLAND. No, indeed.

MRS. MORLAND. I disagree. You two try if you can look at this picture without laughing.

(*They are unable to stand the test.*)

MR. MORLAND. I think I can say that I enjoy a joke as much as ever.

MRS. MORLAND. You light-hearted old man!

MR. MORLAND (*humorously*). Not so old, Fanny. Please to remember that I am two months younger than you.

MRS. MORLAND. How can I forget it when you have been casting it up against me all our married life?

MR. MORLAND (*not without curiosity*). Fanny and I are seventy-three; you are a bit younger, George, I think?

MR. AMY. Oh yes, oh dear yes.

MR. MORLAND. You never say precisely what your age is.

MR. AMY. I am in the late sixties. I am sure I have told you that before.

MR. MORLAND. It seems to me you have been in the sixties longer than it is usual to be in them.

MRS. MORLAND (*with her needles*). James!

MR. MORLAND. No offence, George. I was only going to say that at seventy-three I certainly don't feel my age. How do you feel, George, at—at sixty-six? (*More loudly, as if* MR. AMY *were a little deaf.*) Do you feel your sixty-six years?

MR. AMY (*testily*). I am more than sixty-six. But I certainly don't feel my age. It was only last winter that I learned to skate.

MR. MORLAND. I still go out with the hounds. You forgot to come last time, George.

MR. AMY. If you are implying anything against my memory, James.

MR. MORLAND (*peering through his glasses*). What do you say?

MR. AMY. I was saying that I have never used glasses in my life.

MR. MORLAND. If I wear glasses occasionally it certainly isn't because there is anything defective in my eyesight. But the type used by newspapers nowadays is so vile—

MR. AMY. There I agree with you. Especially Bradshaw.

MR. MORLAND (*not hearing him*). I say the

type used by newspapers of to-day is vile. Don't you think so?

MR. AMY. I have just said so. (*Pleasantly*) You are getting rather dull of hearing, James.

MR. MORLAND. I am? I like that, George! Why, I have constantly to shout to you nowadays.

MR. AMY. What annoys me is not that you are a little deaf, you can't help that. But from the nature of your replies I often see that you are pretending to have heard what I said when you did not. That is rather vain, James.

MR. MORLAND. Vain! Now you brought this on yourself, George. I have got something here I might well be vain of, and I meant not to show it to you because it will make you squirm.

(MRS. MORLAND *taps warningly*.)

MR. MORLAND. I didn't mean that, George. I am sure that you will be delighted. What do you think of this?

(*He produces a water-colour which his friend examines at arm's length.*)

Let me hold it out for you, as your arms are so short.

(*The offer is declined.*)

MR. AMY (*with a sinking*). Very nice. What do you call it?

MR. MORLAND. Have you any doubt? I haven't the slightest. I am sure that it is an early Turner.

MR. AMY (*paling*). Turner!

MR. MORLAND. What else can it be? Holman suggested a Gurton or even a Dayes. Absurd! Why, Dayes was only a glorified drawing-master. I flatter myself I can't make a mistake about a Turner. There is something about a Turner difficult to define, but unmistakable, an absolute something. It is a charming view, too; Kirkstall Abbey obviously.

MR. AMY. Rivaulx, I am convinced.

MR. MORLAND. I say Kirkstall.

MRS. MORLAND (*with her needles*). James!

MR. MORLAND. Well, you may be right, the place doesn't matter.

MR. AMY. There is an engraving of Rivaulx in that Copperplate Magazine we were looking at. (*He turns up the page.*) I have got it, Rivaulx. (*He brightens.*) Why, this is funny. It is an engraving of that very picture. Hello,

hello, hello. (*Examining it through his private glass.*) And it is signed E. Dayes.

> (MR. MORLAND *holds the sketch so close to him that it brushes his eyelashes.*)

I wouldn't eat it, James. So it is by Dayes, the drawing-master, after all. I am sorry you have had this disappointment.

> (MRS. MORLAND *taps warningly, but her husband is now possessed.*)

MR. MORLAND. You sixty-six, Mr. Amy, you sixty-six!

MR. AMY. James, this is very painful. Your chagrin I can well understand, but surely your sense of manhood—I regret that I have outstayed my welcome. I bid you good afternoon. Thank you, Mrs. Morland, for your unvarying hospitality.

MRS. MORLAND. I shall see you into your coat, George.

MR. AMY. It is very kind of you, but I need no one to see me into my coat.

MR. MORLAND. You will never see your way into it by yourself.

> (*This unworthy remark is perhaps not*

heard, for MRS. MORLAND *succeeds once more in bringing the guest back.*)

MR. AMY. James, I cannot leave this friendly house in wrath.

MR. MORLAND. I am an irascible old beggar, George. What I should do without you—

MR. AMY. Or I without you. Or either of us without that little old dear, to whom we are a never-failing source of mirth.

(*The little old dear curtseys, looking very frail as she does so.*)

Tell Simon when he comes that I shall be in to see him to-morrow. Good-bye, Fanny; I suppose you think of the pair of us as in our second childhood?

MRS. MORLAND. Not your second, George. I have never known any men who have quite passed their first.

(*He goes smiling.*)

MR. MORLAND (*ruminating by the fire*). He is a good fellow, George, but how touchy he is about his age. And he has a way of tottering off to sleep while one is talking to him.

MRS. MORLAND. He is not the only one of us who does that.

(*She is standing by the window.*)

MR. MORLAND. What are you thinking about, Fanny?

MRS. MORLAND. I was thinking about the apple-tree, and that you have given the order for its destruction.

MR. MORLAND. It must come down. It is becoming a danger, might fall on some one down there any day.

MRS. MORLAND. I quite see that it has to go. (*She can speak of* MARY ROSE *without a tremor now.*) But her tree! How often she made it a ladder from this room to the ground.

(MR. MORLAND *does not ask who, but he very nearly does so.*)

MR. MORLAND. Oh yes, of course. Did she use to climb the apple-tree? Yes, I think she did.

(*He goes to his wife, as it were for protection.*)

MRS. MORLAND (*not failing him*). Had you forgotten that also, James?

MR. MORLAND. I am afraid I forget a lot of things.

MRS. MORLAND. Just as well.

MR. MORLAND. It is so long since she—how long is it, Fanny?

MRS. MORLAND. Twenty-five years, a third of our lifetime. It will soon be dark; I can see the twilight running across the fields. Draw the curtains, dear.

(*He does so and turns on the lights; they are electric lights now.*)

Simon's train must be nearly due, is it not?

MR. MORLAND. In ten minutes or so. Did you forward his telegram?

MRS. MORLAND. No, I thought he would probably get it sooner if I kept it here.

MR. MORLAND. I dare say. (*He joins her on the sofa, and she sees that he is troubled.*)

MRS. MORLAND. What is it, dear?

MR. MORLAND. I am afraid I was rather thoughtless about the apple-tree, Fanny. I hurt you.

MRS. MORLAND (*brightly*). Such nonsense. Have another pipe, James.

MR. MORLAND (*doggedly*). I will not have another pipe. I hereby undertake to give up smoking for a week as a punishment to myself. (*His breast swells a little.*)

MRS. MORLAND. You will regret this, you know.

MR. MORLAND (*his breast ceasing to swell*). Why is my heart not broken? If I had been a man of real feeling it would have broken twenty-five years ago, just as yours did.

MRS. MORLAND. Mine didn't, dear.

MR. MORLAND. In a way it did. As for me, at the time I thought I could never raise my head again, but there is a deal of the old Adam in me still. I ride and shoot and laugh and give pompous decisions on the bench and wrangle with old George as if nothing much had happened to me. I never think of the island now; I dare say I could go back there and fish. (*He finds that despite his outburst his hand has strayed towards his tobacco-pouch.*) See what I am doing! (*He casts his pouch aside as if it were the culprit.*) I am a man enamoured of myself. Why, I have actually been considering, Fanny, whether I should have another dress suit.

MRS. MORLAND (*picking up the pouch*). And why shouldn't you?

MR. MORLAND. At my age! Fanny, this should be put on my tombstone: 'In spite of some adversity he remained a lively old blade to the end.'

MRS. MORLAND. Perhaps that would be a rather creditable epitaph for any man, James, who has gone through as much as you have. What better encouragement to the young than to be able to tell them that happiness keeps breaking through? (*She puts the pipe, which she has been filling, in his mouth.*)

MR. MORLAND. If I smoke, Fanny, I shall despise myself more than ever.

MRS. MORLAND. To please me.

MR. MORLAND (*as she holds the light*). I don't feel easy about it, not at all easy. (*With a happy thought.*) At any rate, I won't get the dress suit.

MRS. MORLAND. Your dress suit is shining like a mirror.

MR. MORLAND. Isn't it! I thought of a jacket suit only. The V-shaped waistcoat seems to be what they are all wearing now.

MRS. MORLAND. Would you have braid on the trousers?

MR. MORLAND. I was wondering. You see— Oh, Fanny, you are just humouring me.

MRS. MORLAND. Not at all. And as for the old Adam in you, dear Adam, there is still something of the old Eve in me. Our trip to Switzerland two years ago with Simon, I enjoyed every hour of it. The little card parties here, am I not called the noisy one; think of the girls I have chaperoned and teased and laughed with, just as if I had never had a girl myself.

MR. MORLAND. Your brightness hasn't been all pretence?

MRS. MORLAND. No, indeed; I have passed through the valley of the shadow, dear, but I can say thankfully that I have come out again into the sunlight. (*A little tremulously*) I suppose it is all to the good that as the years go by the dead should recede farther from us.

MR. MORLAND. Some say they don't.

MRS. MORLAND. You and I know better, James.

MR. MORLAND. Up there in the misty

Hebrides I dare say they think of her as on the island still. Fanny, how long is it since—since you half thought *that* yourself?

MRS. MORLAND. Ever so many years. Perhaps not the first year. I did cling for a time—

MR. MORLAND. The neighbours here didn't like it.

MRS. MORLAND. She wasn't their Mary Rose, you see.

MR. MORLAND. And yet her first disappearance—

MRS. MORLAND. It is all unfathomable. It is as if Mary Rose was just something beautiful that you and I and Simon had dreamt together. You have forgotten much, but so have I. Even that room—(*she looks towards the little door*)—that was hers and her child's during all her short married life—I often go into it now without remembering that it was theirs.

MR. MORLAND. It is strange. It is rather terrible. You are pretty nigh forgotten, Mary Rose.

MRS. MORLAND. That isn't true, dear. Mary Rose belongs to the past, and we have to live in the present, for a very little longer. Just a little longer, and then we shall understand all. Even if we could drag her back to tell us now what these things mean, I think it would be a shame.

MR. MORLAND. Yes, I suppose so. Do you think Simon is a philosopher about it also?

MRS. MORLAND. Don't be bitter, James, to your old wife. Simon was very fond of her. He was a true lover.

MR. MORLAND. Was, was! Is it all 'was' about Mary Rose?

MRS. MORLAND. It just has to be. He had all the clever ones of the day advising, suggesting, probing. He went back to the island every year for a long time.

MR. MORLAND. Yes, and then he missed a year, and that somehow ended it.

MRS. MORLAND. He never married again. Most men would.

MR. MORLAND. His work took her place. What a jolly, hearty fellow he is.

MRS. MORLAND. If you mean he isn't heartbroken, he isn't. Mercifully the wound has healed.

MR. MORLAND. I am not criticising, Fanny. I suppose any one who came back after twenty-five years—however much they had been loved—it might—we—should we know what to say to them, Fanny?

MRS. MORLAND. Don't, James. (*She rises.*) Simon is late, isn't he?

MR. MORLAND. Very little. I heard the train a short time ago, and he might be here—just—if he had the luck to find a cab. But not if he is walking across the fields.

MRS. MORLAND. Listen!

MR. MORLAND. Yes, wheels. That is probably Simon. He had got a cab.

MRS. MORLAND. I do hope he won't laugh at me for having lit a fire in his room.

MR. MORLAND (*with masculine humour*). I hope you put him out some bed-socks.

MRS. MORLAND (*eagerly*). Do you think he would let me? You wretch!

> (*She hurries out and returns in* SIMON'S *arms.*
>
> *He is in a greatcoat and mufti. He looks his years, grizzled with grey hair and not*

very much of it, and the tuft is gone. He is heavier and more commanding, full of vigour, a rollicking sea-dog for the moment, but it is a face that could be stern to harshness.)

SIMON (*saluting*). Come aboard, sir.

MRS. MORLAND. Let me down, you great bear. You know how I hate to be rumpled.

MR. MORLAND. Not she, loves it. Always did. Get off your greatcoat, Simon. Down with it anywhere.

MRS. MORLAND (*fussing delightedly*). How cold your hands are. Come nearer to the fire.

MR. MORLAND. He is looking fit, though.

SIMON. We need to be fit—these days.

MRS. MORLAND. So nice to have you again. You do like duck, don't you? The train was late, wasn't it?

SIMON. A few minutes only. I made a selfish bolt for the one cab, and got it.

MR. MORLAND. We thought you might be walking across the fields.

SIMON. No, I left the fields to the two other people who got out of the train. One of them was a lady; I thought something about her walk was familiar to me, but it was darkish, and I didn't make her out.

MRS. MORLAND. Bertha Colinton, I expect. She was in London to-day.

SIMON. If I had thought it was Mrs. Colinton I would have offered her a lift. (*For a moment he gleams boyishly like the young husband of other days.*) Mother, I have news; I have got the *Bellerophon*, honest Injun!

MRS. MORLAND. The very ship you wanted.

SIMON. Rather.

MR. MORLAND. Bravo, Simon.

SIMON. It is like realising the ambition of one's life. I'm one of the lucky folk, I admit.

(*He says this, and neither of them notices it as a strange remark.*)

MR. MORLAND (*twinkling*). Beastly life, a sailor's.

SIMON (*cordially*). Beastly. I have loathed it ever since I slept in the old *Britannia*, with my feet out at the port-hole to give them air. We all slept that way; must have been a pretty sight from the water. Oh, a beast of a life, but

I wouldn't exchange it for any other in the world. (*Lowering*) And if this war does come—

MR. MORLAND (*characteristically*). It won't, I'm sure.

SIMON. I dare say not. But they say—however.

MRS. MORLAND. Simon, I had forgotten. There is a telegram for you.

SIMON. Avaunt! I do trust it is not recalling me. I had hoped for at least five clear days.

MRS. MORLAND (*giving it to him*). We didn't open it.

SIMON. Two to one it is recalling me.

MRS. MORLAND. It came two days ago. I don't like them, Simon, never did; they have broken so many hearts.

SIMON. They have made many a heart glad too. It may be from my Harry—at last. Mother, do you think I was sometimes a bit harsh to him?

MRS. MORLAND. I think you sometimes were, my son.

MR. MORLAND. Open it, Simon.

(SIMON *opens the telegram and many unseen devils steal into the room.*)

MRS. MORLAND (*shrinking from his face*).
It can't be so bad as that. We are all here,
Simon.

> (*For a moment he has not been here himself,
> he has been on an island. He is a good
> son to* MRS. MORLAND *now, thinking of her
> only, placing her on the sofa, going on his
> knees beside her and stroking her kind face.
> Her arms go out to her husband, who has
> been reading the telegram.*)

MR. MORLAND (*dazed*). Can't be, can't be!

SIMON (*like some better father than he perhaps
has been*). It is all right, Mother. Don't you
be afraid. It is good news. You are a brave
one, you have come through much, you will be
brave for another minute, won't you?

> (*She nods, with a frightened smile.*)

Mother dear, it is Mary Rose.

MR. MORLAND. It can't be true. It is too—
too glorious to be true.

MRS. MORLAND. Glorious? Is my Mary Rose
alive?

SIMON. It is all right, all right. I wouldn't
say it, surely, if it wasn't true. Mary Rose

has come back. The telegram is from Cameron. You remember who he was. He is minister there now. Hold my hand, and I'll read it. 'Your wife has come back. She was found to-day on the island. I am bringing her to you. She is quite well, but you will all have to be very careful.'

MRS. MORLAND. Simon, can it be?

SIMON. I believe it absolutely. Cameron would not deceive me.

MR. MORLAND. He might be deceived himself; he was a mere acquaintance.

SIMON. I am sure it is true. He knew her by sight as well as any of us.

MR. MORLAND. But after twenty-five years!

SIMON. Do you think I wouldn't know her after twenty-five years?

MRS. MORLAND. My—my—she will be—very changed.

SIMON. However changed, Mother, wouldn't I know my Mary Rose at once! Her hair may be as grey as mine—her face—her little figure—her pretty ways—though they were all gone, don't you think I would know Mary Rose at once? (*He is suddenly stricken with a painful thought.*) Oh, my God, I saw her, and I didn't know her!

MRS. MORLAND. Simon!

SIMON. It had been Cameron with her. They must have come in my train. Mother, it was she I saw going across the fields—her little walk when she was excited, half a run, I recognised it, but I didn't remember it was hers.

(*Those unseen devils chuckle.*)

MR. MORLAND. It was getting dark.

SIMON (*slowly*). Mary Rose is coming across the fields.

(*He goes out.* MORLAND *peers weakly through the window curtains.* MRS. MOR-LAND *goes on her knees to pray.*)

MR. MORLAND. It is rather dark. I—I shouldn't wonder though there was a touch of frost to-night. I wish I was more use.

(CAMERON *enters, a bearded clergyman now.*)

MRS. MORLAND. Mr. Cameron? Tell us quickly, Mr. Cameron, is it true?

CAMERON. It iss true, ma'am. Mr. Blake met us at the gate and he iss with her now. I hurried on to tell you the things necessary. It iss good for her you should know them at once.

MRS. MORLAND. Please, quick.

CAMERON. You must be prepared to find her—different.

MRS. MORLAND. We are all different. Her age—

CAMERON. I mean, Mrs. Morland, different from what you expect. She iss not different as we are different. They will be saying she iss just as she was on the day she went away.

(MRS. MORLAND *shrinks*.)

These five-and-twenty years, she will be thinking they were just an hour in which Mr. Blake and I had left her in some incomprehensible jest.

MRS. MORLAND. James, just as it was before!

MR. MORLAND. But when you told her the truth?

CAMERON. She will not have it.

MRS. MORLAND. She must have seen how much older you are.

CAMERON. She does not know me, ma'am, as the boy who was with her that day. When she did not recognise me I thought it best—she was so troubled already—not to tell her.

MR. MORLAND (*appealing*). But now that she has seen Simon. His appearance, his grey hair—when she saw him she would know.

CAMERON (*unhappy*). I am not sure; it iss dark out there.

MR. MORLAND. She must have known that he would never have left her and come home.

CAMERON. That secretly troubles her, but she will not speak of it. There iss some terrible dread lying on her heart.

MR. MORLAND. A dread?

MRS. MORLAND. Harry. James, if she should think that Harry is still a child!

CAMERON. I never heard what became of the boy.

MRS. MORLAND. He ran away to sea when he was twelve years old. We had a few letters from Australia, very few; we don't know where he is now.

MR. MORLAND. How was she found, Mr. Cameron?

CAMERON. Two men fishing from a boat saw

her. She was asleep by the shore at the very spot where Mr. Blake made a fire so long ago. There was a rowan-tree beside it. At first they were afraid to land, but they did. They said there was such a joy on her face as she slept that it was a shame to waken her.

MR. MORLAND. Joy?

CAMERON. That iss so, sir. I have sometimes thought—

(There is a gleeful clattering on the stairs of some one to whom they must be familiar; and if her father and mother have doubted they know now before they see her that MARY ROSE *has come back. She enters. She is just as we saw her last except that we cannot see her quite so clearly. She is leaping towards her mother in the old impulsive way and the mother responds in her way, but something steps between them.)*

MARY ROSE (*puzzled*). What is it?

(*It is the years.*)

MRS. MORLAND. My love.

MR. MORLAND. Mary Rose.

MARY ROSE. Father.

> (*But the obstacle is still there. She turns timidly to* SIMON, *who has come in with her.*)

What is it, Simon?

> (*She goes confidently to him till she sees what the years have done with him. She shakes now.*)

SIMON. My beloved wife.

> (*He takes her in his arms and so does her mother, and she is glad to be there, but it is not of them she is thinking, and soon she softly disengages herself.*)

MR. MORLAND. We are so glad you—had you a comfortable journey, Mary Rose? You would like a cup of tea, wouldn't you? Is there anything *I* can do?

> (MARY ROSE'S *eyes go from him to the little door at the back.*)

MARY ROSE (*coaxingly to her father*). Tell me.

MR. MORLAND. Tell you what, dear?

MARY ROSE (*appealing to* CAMERON). You?

> (*He presses her hand and turns away. She*

goes to SIMON *and makes much of him, cajoling him.*)

Simon, my Simon. Be nice to me, Simon. Be nice to me, dear Simon, and tell me.

SIMON. Dearest love, since I lost you—it was a long time ago—

MARY ROSE (*petulant*). It wasn't—please, it wasn't. (*She goes to her mother.*) Tell me, my mother dear.

MR. MORLAND. I don't know what she wants to be told.

MRS. MORLAND. I know.

MARY ROSE (*an unhappy child*). Where is my baby?

> (*They cannot face her, and she goes to seek an answer from the room that lies beyond the little door. Her mother and husband follow her.*
>
> MR. MORLAND *and* CAMERON *left alone are very conscious of what may be going on in that inner room.*)

MR. MORLAND. Have you been in this part of the country before, Mr. Cameron?

CAMERON. I haf not, sir. It iss my first

visit to England. You cannot hear the sea in this house at all, which iss very strange to me.

MR. MORLAND. If I might show you our Downs—

CAMERON. I thank you, Mr. Morland, but—in such circumstances do not trouble about me at all.

(*They listen.*)

MR. MORLAND. I do not know if you are interested in prints. I have a pencil sketch by Cousins—undoubtedly genuine—

CAMERON. I regret my ignorance on the subject. This matter, so strange—so inexplicable—

MR. MORLAND. Please don't talk of it to me, sir. I am—an old man. I have been so occupied all my life with little things—very pleasant —I cannot cope—cannot cope—

(*A hand is placed on his shoulder so sympathetically that he dares to ask a question.*)

Do you think she should have come back, Mr. Cameron?

(*The stage darkens and they are blotted out.
Into this darkness* MRS. OTERY *enters with
a candle, and we see that the scene has
changed to the dismantled room of the first
act.* HARRY *is sunk in the chair as we
last saw him.*)

MRS. OTERY (*who in her other hand has a large
cup and saucer*). Here is your tea, mister. Are
you sitting in the dark? I haven't been more
than the ten minutes I promised you. I was—

(*She stops short, struck by his appearance.
She holds the candle nearer him. He is
staring wide-eyed into the fire, motionless.*)

What is the matter, mister? Here is the tea,
mister.

(*He looks at her blankly.*)

I have brought you a cup of tea, I have just
been the ten minutes.

HARRY (*rising*). Wait a mo.

(*He looks about him, like one taking his
bearings.*)

Gimme the tea. That's better. Thank you,
missis.

MRS. OTERY. Have you seen anything?

HARRY. See here, as I sat in that chair—I wasn't sleeping, mind you—it's no dream—but things of the far past connected with this old house—things I knew naught of—they came crowding out of their holes and gathered round me till I saw—I saw them all so clear that I don't know what to think, woman. (*He is a grave man now.*) Never mind about that. Tell me about this—ghost.

MRS. OTERY. It's no concern of yours.

HARRY. Yes, it is some concern of mine. The folk that used to live here—the Morlands—

MRS. OTERY. That was the name. I suppose you heard it in the village?

HARRY. I have heard it all my days. It is one of the names I bear. I am one of the family.

MRS. OTERY. I suspicioned that.

HARRY. I suppose that is what made them come to me as I sat here. Tell me about them.

MRS. OTERY. It is little I know. They were dead and gone before my time, the old man and his wife.

HARRY. It's not them I am asking you about.

MRS. OTERY. They had a son-in-law, a sailor.

The war made a great man of him before it drowned him.

HARRY. I know that; he was my father. Hard I used to think him, but I know better now. Go on, there's the other one.

MRS. OTERY (*reluctantly*). That was all.

HARRY. There is one more.

MRS. OTERY. If you must speak of her, she is dead too. I never saw her in life.

HARRY. Where is she buried?

MRS. OTERY. Down by the church.

HARRY. Is there a stone?

MRS. OTERY. Yes.

HARRY. Does it say her age?

MRS. OTERY. No.

HARRY. Is that holy spot well taken care of?

MRS. OTERY. You can see for yourself.

HARRY. I will see for myself. And so it is her ghost that haunts this house?

> (*She makes no answer. He struggles with himself.*)

There is no such thing as ghosts. And yet— Is it true about folk having lived in this house and left in a hurry?

MRS. OTERY. It's true.

HARRY. Because of a ghost—a thing that can't be.

MRS. OTERY. When I came in your eyes were staring; I thought you had seen her.

HARRY. Have you ever seen her yourself?

(*She shivers.*)

Where? In this room?

(*She looks at the little door.*)

In there? Has she ever been seen out of that room?

MRS. OTERY. All over the house, in every room and on the stairs. I tell you I've met her on the stairs, and she drew back to let me pass and said 'Good evening' too, timid-like, and at another time she has gone by me like a rush of wind.

HARRY. What is she like? Is she dressed in white? They are allus dressed in white, aren't they?

MRS. OTERY. She looks just like you or me. But for all that she's as light as air. I've seen—things.

HARRY. You look like it, too. But she is harmless, it seems?

MRS. OTERY. There's some wouldn't say that; them that left in a hurry. If she thought you were keeping it from her she would do you a mischief.

HARRY. Keeping what from her?

MRS. OTERY. Whatever it is she prowls about this cold house searching for, searching, searching. I don't know what it is.

HARRY (*grimly*). Maybe I could tell you. I dare say I could even put her in the way of finding him.

MRS. OTERY. Then I wish to God you would, and let her rest.

HARRY. My old dear, there are worse things than not finding what you are looking for; there is finding them so different from what you had hoped. (*He moves about.*) A ghost. Oh no—and yet, and yet— See here, I am going into that room.

MRS. OTERY. As you like; I care not.

HARRY. I'll burst open the door.

MRS. OTERY. No need; it's not locked; I cheated you about that.

HARRY. But I tried it and it wouldn't open.

(MRS. OTERY *is very unhappy.*)

You think she is in there?

MRS. OTERY. She may be.

HARRY (*taking a deep breath*). Give me air.

(*He throws open the window and we see that it is a night of stars.*)

Leave me here now. I have a call to make.

MRS. OTERY (*hesitating*). I dunno. You think you're in no danger, but—

HARRY. That is how it is to be, missis. Just ten minutes you were out of the room, did you say?

MRS. OTERY. That was all.

HARRY. God!

(*She leaves him. After a moment's irresolution he sets off upon his quest carrying the candle, which takes with it all the light of the room. He is visible on the other side of the darkness, in the little passage and opening the door beyond. He returns, and now we see the pale ghost of* MARY ROSE *standing in the middle of the room, as if made out of the light he has brought back with him.*)

MARY ROSE (*bowing to him timidly*). Have you come to buy the house?

HARRY (*more startled by his own voice than by hers*). Not me.

MARY ROSE. It is a very nice house. (*Doubtfully*) Isn't it?

HARRY. It was a nice house once.

MARY ROSE (*pleased*). Wasn't it! (*Suspiciously*) Did you know this house?

HARRY. When I was a young shaver.

MARY ROSE. Young? Was it you who laughed?

HARRY. When was that?

MARY ROSE (*puzzled*). There was once some one who laughed in this house. Don't you think laughter is a very pretty sound?

HARRY (*out of his depths*). Is it? I dare say. I never thought about it.

MARY ROSE. You are quite old.

HARRY. I'm getting on.

MARY ROSE (*confidentially*). Would you mind telling me why every one is so old? I don't know you, do I?

HARRY. I wonder. Take a look. You might

have seen me in the old days—playing about—
outside in the garden—or even inside.

MARY ROSE. You—you are not Simon, are
you?

HARRY. No. (*Venturing*) My name is Harry.

MARY ROSE (*stiffening*). *I* don't think so. I
strongly object to your saying that.

HARRY. I'm a queer sort of cove, and I
would like to hear you call me Harry.

MARY ROSE (*firmly*). I decline. I regret, but
I absolutely decline.

HARRY. No offence.

MARY ROSE. I think you are sorry for me.

HARRY. I am that.

MARY ROSE. I am sorry for me, too.

HARRY (*desperately desirous to help her*). If
only there was something I— I know nothing
about ghosts—not a thing; can they sit down?
Could you—?

(*He turns the chair toward her.*)

MARY ROSE. That is your chair.

HARRY. What do you mean by that?

MARY ROSE. That is where you were
sitting.

HARRY. Were you in this room when I was sitting there?

MARY ROSE. I came in to look at you.

(*A sudden thought makes him cross with the candle to where he had left his knife. It is gone.*)

HARRY. Where is my knife? Were you standing looking at me with my knife in your hand?

(*She is sullenly silent.*)

Give me my knife.

(*She gives it to him.*)

What made you take it?

MARY ROSE. I thought you were perhaps the one.

HARRY. The one?

MARY ROSE. The one who stole him from me.

HARRY. I see. Godsake, in a sort of way I suppose I am.

(*He sits in the chair.*)

MARY ROSE. Give him back to me.

HARRY. I wish I could. But I'm doubting he is gone beyond recall.

MARY ROSE (*unexpectedly*). Who is he?

HARRY. Do you mean you have forgotten who it is you are searching for?

MARY ROSE. I knew once. It is such a long time ago. I am so tired; please can I go away and play now?

HARRY. Go away? Where? You mean back to that—that place?

(*She nods.*)

What sort of a place is it? Is it good to be there?

MARY ROSE. Lovely, lovely, lovely.

HARRY. It's not just the island, is it, that's so lovely, lovely?

(*She is perplexed.*)

Have you forgotten the island too?

MARY ROSE. I am sorry.

HARRY. The island, the place where you heard the call.

MARY ROSE. What is that?

HARRY. You have even forgotten the call! (*With vision*) As far as I can make out, it was as if, in a way, there were two kinds of dogs out hunting you—the good and the bad.

MARY ROSE (*who thinks he is chiding her*). Please don't be cross with me.

HARRY. I am far from cross with you. I

begin to think it was the good dogs that got you. Are they ghosts in that place?

MARY ROSE (*with surprising certainty*). No.

HARRY. You are sure?

MARY ROSE. Honest Injun.

HARRY. What fairly does me is, if the place is so lovely, what made you leave it?

MARY ROSE (*frightened*). I don't know.

HARRY. Do you think you could have fallen out?

MARY ROSE. I don't know. (*She thinks his power is great.*) Please, I don't want to be a ghost any more.

HARRY. As far as I can see, if you wasn't a ghost there you made yourself one by coming back. But it's no use your expecting me to be able to help you. (*She droops at this and he holds out his arms.*) Come to me, ghostie; I wish you would.

MARY ROSE (*prim again*). Certainly not.

HARRY. If you come, I'll try to help you.

(*She goes at once and sits on his knee.*)
See here, when I was sitting by the fire alone I seemed to hear you as you once were saying

that some day when he was a man you would like to sit on your Harry's knee.

MARY ROSE (*vaguely quoting she knows not whom*). The loveliest time of all will be when he is a man and takes me on his knee instead of my taking him on mine.

HARRY. Do you see who I am now?

MARY ROSE. Nice man.

HARRY. Is that all you know about me?

MARY ROSE. Yes.

HARRY. There is a name I would like to call you by, but my best course is not to worry you. Poor soul, I wonder if there was ever a man with a ghost on his knee before.

MARY ROSE. I don't know.

HARRY. Seems to me you 're feared of being a ghost. I dare say, to a timid thing, being a ghost is worse than seeing them.

MARY ROSE. Yes.

HARRY. Is it lonely being a ghost?

MARY ROSE. Yes.

HARRY. Do you know any other ghosts?

MARY ROSE. No.

HARRY. Would you like to know other ghosts?

MARY ROSE. Yes.

HARRY. I can understand that. And now you would like to go away and play?

MARY ROSE. Please.

HARRY. In this cold house, when you should be searching, do you sometimes play by yourself instead?

MARY ROSE (*whispering*). Don't tell.

HARRY. Not me. You're a pretty thing. What beautiful shoes you have.

(*She holds out her feet complacently.*)

MARY ROSE. Nice buckles.

HARRY. I like your hair.

MARY ROSE. Pretty hair.

HARRY. Do you mind the tuft that used to stand up at the back of — of Simon's head?

MARY ROSE (*merrily*). Naughty tuft.

HARRY. I have one like that.

MARY ROSE (*smoothing it down*). Oh dear, oh dear, what a naughty tuft.

HARRY. My name is Harry.

MARY ROSE (*liking the pretty sound*). Harry, Harry, Harry, Harry.

HARRY. But you don't know what Harry I am.

MARY ROSE. No.

HARRY. And this brings us no nearer what's to be done with you. I would willingly stay here though I have my clearing in Australy, but you're just a ghost. They say there are ways of laying ghosts, but I am so ignorant.

MARY ROSE (*imploringly*). Tell me.

HARRY. I wish I could; you are even more ignorant than I am.

MARY ROSE. Tell me.

HARRY. All I know about them for certain is that they are unhappy because they can't find something, and then once they've got the thing they want, they go away happy and never come back.

MARY ROSE. Oh, nice.

HARRY. The one thing clear to me is that you have got that thing at last, but you are too dog-tired to know or care. What you need now is to get back to the place you say is lovely, lovely.

MARY ROSE. Yes, yes.

HARRY. It sounds as if it might be Heaven, or near thereby.

(*She wants him to find out for her.*)
Queer, you that know so much can tell nothing, and them that know nothing can tell so much. If there was any way of getting you to that glory place!

MARY ROSE. Tell me.

HARRY (*desperate*). He would surely send for you, if He wanted you.

MARY ROSE (*crushed*). Yes.

HARRY. It's like as if He had forgotten you.

MARY ROSE. Yes.

HARRY. It's as if nobody wanted you, either there or here.

MARY ROSE. Yes. (*She rises.*) Bad man.

HARRY. It's easy to call me names, but the thing fair beats me. There is nothing I wouldn't do for you, but a mere man is so helpless. How should the likes of me know what to do with a ghost that has lost her way on earth? I wonder if what it means is that you broke some law, just to come back for the sake of—of that Harry? If it was that, it's surely time He overlooked it.

MARY ROSE. Yes.

(*He looks at the open window.*)

HARRY. What a night of stars! Good old glitterers, I dare say they are in the know, but I am thinking you are too small a thing to get a helping hand from them.

MARY ROSE. Yes.

> (*The call is again heard, but there is in it now no unholy sound. It is a celestial music that is calling for Mary Rose, Mary Rose, first in whispers and soon so loudly that, for one who can hear, it is the only sound in the world. Mary Rose, Mary Rose. As it wraps her round, the weary little ghost knows that her long day is done. Her face is shining. The smallest star shoots down as if it were her star sent for her, and with her arms stretched forth to it trustingly she walks out through the window into the empyrean. The music passes with her.* HARRY *hears nothing, but he knows that somehow a prayer has been answered.*)

THE END